TALES

FROM THE LAST DAYS OF

ANATOLIA

TERRY STAVRIDIS

Ordering Information:

Prime Seven Media
518 Landmann St.
Tomah City, WI 54660

Printed in the United States of America

TABLE OF CONTENTS

Ethnic Groups in the Balkans and Asia Minor as of early 1911

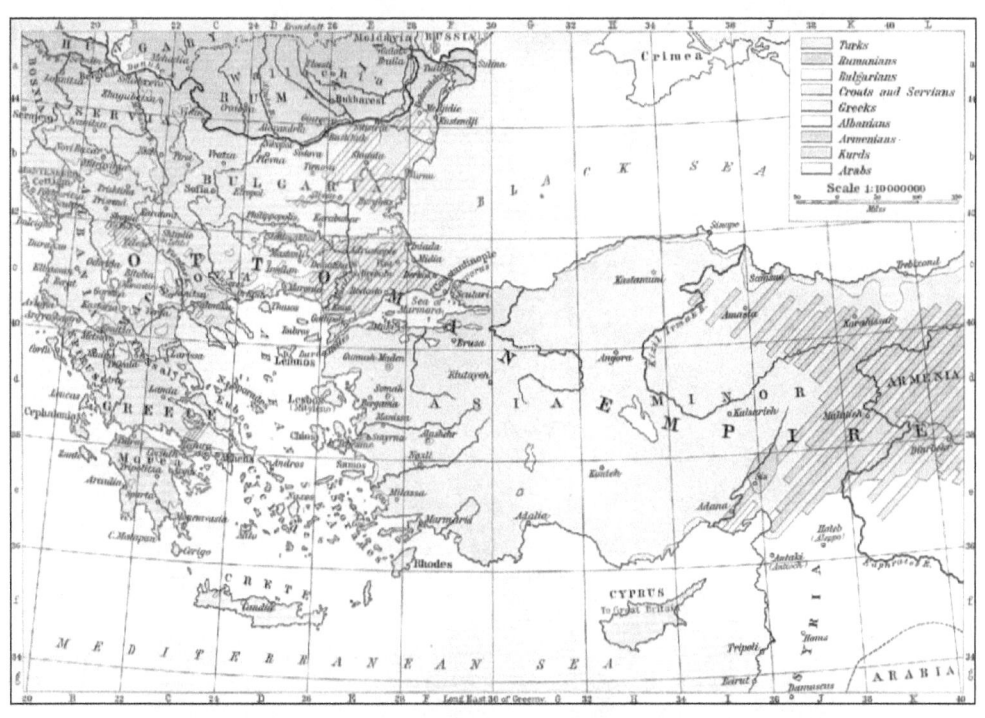

PROLOGUE

Human tyranny, abuse of power and destruction of people have been always part of collective human behaviour. During the first quarter of the 20th century fundamentalist, nationalist and radicalized populist Turkish leaders undertook a systematic national, ethnic, racial and religious campaign of cleansing against the minorities residing in Turkey, predominately, but not exclusively, against Armenians, Greeks and Assyrians. Australian historian Terry Stavridis over the last thirty years made a formidable and gallant effort to record, document, analyze and compile several aspects of this malevolent collective behaviour, which received the size of a genocide. Yet, unfortunately, this appalling misconduct has been perceived by modern Turkish rulers as "an act of war". Their mode of behaviour by these rulers, to consider as legitimate and "balanced" the atrocities committed by their ancestors, simply transplants the sense of culpability and onus on current Turkish leadership, leaving no space for remorse or thoughts for amity and reconciliation.

The first quarter of the 20th century has been one of the most turbulent periods in the Balkan's and Asia Minor's modern history. Continuous inter-ethnic wars, ethnic and political revolutions, coupled by political unrests, military coupes, massive executions as well as insurgents by guerrilla forces, constant inflows of hundreds of thousands fleeing refugees caused by unnecessary vindictiveness and cruelty, scores of massive deaths in organized "labour battalions" during nasty and long death marches though deserts had been partially the outcome of this inter-ethnic tragedy. The defeat and collapse of the Ottoman Empire and the emergence of the Modern Turk nationalists instigated a vicious campaign of retaliation and vengeance against the indigenous Greek population of the Empire and it included massacres, forced deportations, summary expulsions, arbitrary executions, and the destruction of Eastern Orthodox cultural, historical, and religious monuments.

Terry Stavridis an experienced writer, balancing subjectiveness with objectiveness, authored a large volume of Chapters in collective volumes and essays in refereed journal depicting and outlining the aforementioned events from a historical narrative perspective. Over three decades, his history-writing was based on reconstructing series of short-term events, and since the influential work of Leopold von Ranke on professionalising history- writing in the nineteenth century has been associated with Asia Minor empiricism. The historical fiction stories authored by Terry Stavridis and incorporated in this volume allows us to understand the extremes of human behaviour as well as the extent of human suffering as a result of human bellicosity. Stavridis eloquently outlines the various ways of facing, understanding and living with the horrific events in the past. Via these stories the reader will have ample opportunity to understand, appreciate and retain a past that had caused substantial pain and suffering. However, the reader via this historical narrative will also recover optimism and anticipation of human fidelity and comradeship, human heroism and a commitment to duty.

Terry Stavridis should also be commendable for presenting the socio-cultural events on a creditable and empathetic style outlying and co-ordinating the historic time and places, the protagonists, their institutions and cultural aspects as well as the related events unadulterated by nationalistic outbursts or unnecessary biased commentary. The reader will perhaps derive the message that inter-ethnic amity and humanism could prevail even under circumstances of acute human brutality...

Professor Anastasios M. Tamis

INTRODUCTION

I have dedicated my historical research to the Greco-Turkish war 1919-23 for over twenty years. This conflict took place in Asia Minor today, known as Turkey, an area that was inhabited by Ottoman Turks, Greeks, Armenians, Assyrians, Kurds, Circassians, and Arabs. There were times when these ethnic groups lived harmoniously with each other. In times of conflict, the Ottoman Turks and later the

Turkish Nationalists led by Mustapha Kemal Pasha committed atrocities against their Christian populations.

The major European powers viewed the Ottoman Empire as the sick man of Europe. In particular, Great Britain, France, Germany, Russia, and Italy sought economic concessions from the Sultan in the late 19th-early 20th centuries. Each power had its own political and economic agenda in preventing the collapse of the Ottoman state. The British viewed the Ottoman Empire as a bulwark to Russian expansion into the Eastern Mediterranean that could threaten its vital strategic interests in the Suez Canal through the Red Sea and onto its sub-empire in India. The French and British were the largest bondholders in the Ottoman Empire and wanted to ensure that Turks met their financial obligations from the massive loans they borrowed over the 19th century.

When World War 1 started, the Ottoman Empire remained neutral for a short time before casting its lot with the Central Powers, Germany, and Austro-Hungary.

Initially, the Entente- Britain, France, and Russia told the Sultan that nothing would happen to his empire so long as he remained neutral. However, that all changed with the Entente concluding a series of secret agreements to parcel out the Ottoman

Empire into spheres of influence at the end of hostilities.

The Greek Prime Minister, Eleftherios Venizelos, envisioned that Smyrna would be given to Greece at the end of hostilities as its reward for fighting alongside the Entente. Alternatively, King Constantine did not wish Greece's involvement in the Great War. The King dismissed Venizelos over differences in foreign policy. For a short time, Greece had two rival governments, one led by the King in Athens and the other in Salonika under Venizelos. Eventually, the French removed Constantine thus allowing Venizelos to return to power and declaring war against the central powers.

During the Paris Peace Conference of 1919, Venizelos presented his nation's territorial claims with Smyrna as its centerpiece. The Greek occupation of Smyrna sanctioned by Britain, France, and the US in May 1919 set off a series of events that would eventually lead to the defeat of the Greek army by the Kemalists. There is no doubt the Greek landing at Smyrna, with its subsequent death of Turks and destruction of Turkish property, gave birth to the nationalist movement established by Mustapha Kemal.

I examined the tragic events of Asia Minor from a strategic, economic, geopolitical, and humanitarian perspective. I have used countless documents from the British, US, Australian, and League of Nations archives to compose my narratives on this terrible conflict. We see the uprooting and expulsion of thousands of Greeks and

Armenians from their ancestral homelands in Smyrna and Black Sea towns of Samsoun and Trebizond to start new lives in Greece and the United States.

I recently decided to step aside from writing diplomatic and political history and try my hand in writing a fictional tale of Asia Minor based on real events that happened in the early part of the 20th century. It is more comfortable writing conventional history using official documents than recording fictional history where one has to use historical imagination to recreate events as seen through the eyes of the fictional characters.

The use of historical imagination to recreate the past is not easy, as one has to put themselves in the place of the fictional character as to how they viewed the events unfolding before their eyes. These individuals were witnesses to earth- shattering events that shaped the political landscape of the Near East and changed their lives forever. These fictional characters enjoyed rich, comfortable lifestyles before the defeat of the Greek army and losing everything in the end. They became refugees taking with them very few personal possessions to their new place of residence. Life was not easy at the start, but with determination, perseverance, and persistence managed to rebuild their lives.

This is an expanded version with additional new short stories revolving around fictional characters who were participants and witnesses to actual events that occurred in Asia Minor, 1900-23. Their stories detail massacre, ethnic cleansing, genocide, expulsion, uprooting, war, nationalism, xenophobia, discrimination, and the involvement of great powers in Asia Minor.

I decided to give a voice to the history of the below movement, i.e., ordinary people who are mostly are ignored in historical accounts. Most historical accounts focus on significant figures such as kings, prime ministers, queens, popes, presidents, generals, and captains of industry. In this case, I have given a voice to ordinary folks. The fictional survivors kept personal diaries recording momentous historical events that they experienced. These events were recorded mainly after the fact meaning that there may be a discrepancy in their accounts involving that memory can play tricks.

CHAPTER 1

MIHALIS VEZIRIS: MY EARLY YEARS

My name is Mihalis Veziris. I was born to Greek Smyrniotes parents: Manolis and Aphrodite Veziris (nee Papadakis) in 1900. Our father and mother were born in 1860 and 1865 and married in May 1885. My three siblings George Maria, and Alexandra, were born in 1890, 1905, and 1906 respectively. Manolis inherited a carpet factory from his father, Iacovos, who died in 1900, which he ran until September 1922.

My grandfather Iacavos was born into a middle-class family in a small village outside of Smyrna in 1830. His father was a respected country doctor who traveled to nearby villages looking after his patients' needs. Many of his patients thought of him as a miracle worker. Iacavos worked as a clerk for Papamihail Brothers, who owned a small carpet factory in Smyrna. Grandfather was an astute, observant individual who quickly learned about the business. He saved his money and eventually bought his carpet factory in 1860. Our family fortune was built upon his initial hard work.

My mother's family originally came from Mytilini to Smyrna around 1840. They were poor but worked hard, saving their money. Eventually, my maternal grandfather, Alexandros Papadakis, opened a small store selling clothes, utensils, and local foodstuffs. His three daughters- Aphrodite (my mother), Persephone, and Maria, who were brought up in a very strict household. He used to hit his daughters when they disobeyed him. Alexandros was unhappy when my mother was courting my father. I don't know why he disliked him. Anyway, mom and dad finally got married, which Alexandros could nothing about except give his "blessing." Our maternal grandmother, Aliki, liked my father but was afraid to stand up to her husband. Alexandros only attended the church service because he had to give the bride away but never came to our parents' wedding reception.

During the first year of marriage of my parents' marriage, Alexandros frequently intervened in their lives. However, our mother warned him that his continuing interference would lead to the severing of family ties. Alexandros thought that mother was joking, but she wasn't. One day he came to our parent's house to say that he disapproved of the friends they associated with and also the way mother dressed. Mother loved wearing the latest Parisienne fashions. My mother could take it no more and finally told Alexandros to leave and never come back. They never saw each other again. It was sad that both never reconciled their differences. I never got to know my relatives on my mother's side of the family.

We lived in Bournabat, a suburb of Smyrna, where wealthy Greek and Levantine families lived in beautiful stately homes with elegant gardens, manicured lawns, and also hosted their famous garden parties. These parties were attended by the prominent Greek, Armenian, Levantine, and Turkish families of Smyrna. I remember our family invited to these lavish functions, where I got the chance to mix and play with the children of these elite families.

I asked myself, why were we invited to these wealthy houses? It all had to do with our grandfather, who sold carpets to these rich people. He had become terrific friends with some of the Levantine families who invited him into their inner circle. It was considered a privilege to be part of this elite group, which also raised the status of our family's carpet business. It opened doors to develop further his business interests.

Our carpet factory had fierce competition from the Oriental Carpet Factory but always managed to do good business in Smyrna and beyond. My father was very proud of the quality of the carpets he produced and exported them to Athens, London, Marseilles, and Constantinople. We were about to fulfill our first order from the United States but couldn't complete it because of the intervention of the great war.

Our family wasn't as wealthy as the Whittal, Paterson, Woods, Papazoglou, Balatzis, Matirosian, and Edhem families who had lived for generations in Smyrna. Nevertheless, we were very comfortable with servants to do the shopping, cleaning, washing, and gardening. Our mother stayed home, took care of us, and supervised our household. She made sure that every task was performed promptly and treated the servants with respect and kindness.

We employed two Greeks, two Turks, and one Armenian servant. I remember mother telling me that one of the servants named Ahmet needed some time off to look after his very sick wife. She gave him as much time off as he needed to allow her to recuperate from her illness. Mother visited Ahmet's wife by taking some soup to her. Ahmet appreciated my mother's kindness, which he never forgot. The other servants received similar treatment with their family illnesses or religious festivities.

Manolis had two excellent close friends named Stefanos Manos and Christos Papadoukas, who was involved in the import/export business. My father grew up and went to school with them, establishing a lifetime friendship curtailed in September 1922. I also became terrific friends with Manos and Papadoukas children. The former had three sons- Nikolaos, Andreas, and Giorgio whereas the latter had two daughters- Marika and Anna. Our families spent a wonderful summer picnics at Lake Tantalus.

The scenery was simply breathtaking with crystal blue water and surrounded by a wooded forest. Oh! The mountains formed a fantastic backdrop to the lake. We would go rowing and swimming in its crystal blue waters. On other occasions, we would go bike riding and sing songs, which brightened up our day. Many of the affluent families would spend their day of relaxation here. These were wonderful times full of nostalgia and innocence.

My parents enrolled me in the Evangelical School of Smyrna in 1906 and graduated in 1917. This school was open to all children irrespective of race and religion and mainly attended by Greeks. I studied foreign languages (English, Frech, Turkish, and German), history, geography, writing, and geometry. My favorite subject was learning foreign languages, which would stand me in good stead in the coming years. I remember in 1909, the Young Turks in Constantinople passed a law that made the teaching of Turkish compulsory in all schools across the Empire.

The Evangelical school possessed an excellent museum full of archaeological artifacts and a library of some 50,000 volumes. This school rivaled some of the best schools in Athens, and also, the Greek Ministry of Education recognized its graduate certificates. This recognition allowed wealthy Greek Smyrniot families to send their sons to study at the University of Athens without having to undertake the compulsory university entrance examination.

My sisters attended Homer School for Girls, which had been established by a wealthy Frenchman businessman, Jacques Manet, in

1882. They wanted to become teachers. Of course, that was a noble profession, but the poor things never graduated due to events beyond their control. If my sisters had graduated, they would have been able to teach in Greece as well.

By the time I graduated from the Evangelical School, my sisters were in the 5th and 6th grades of primary school, respectively. Both were very bright students, with their teachers predicting a great future ahead of them. They were adamant of becoming school teachers, and our parents fully supported them. I was very proud of my sisters, and sincerely hoped they would fulfill their dreams.

In 1908, two important events happened in my life. The first was the Young Turk revolution in the summer of that year, and George migrating to America. I remember my father feeling so happy when the Young Turks seized power in Constantinople, promising to treat all the Greeks and Armenians equally. He thought that good days were coming at last. However, things changed quickly within a year with the slogan "Turkey for the Turks." My father felt he had been deceived and had some apprehension about our family's future in Turkey. However, the Turkish Governor, Essad Pasha, reassured the Greeks and Armenians that they had nothing to fear so long as he was in charge. That proved reassuring for my father. Our father managed to become good friends with Essad, which also helped our carpet business. Essad was able to get his rich Pasha friends to buy from us. I never found out how our father established his friendship with Essad.

George's decision to go to America caught my family by complete surprise. He had been planning this for some time. A Smyrniot friend who had migrated to America in 1902 convinced George that this was the land of golden opportunity.

George got itchy feet to leave us. George was a restless soul who found it challenging to work in our carpet business. He was the adventurous type who wanted to prove that he could make his luck far away from Smyrna.

On the other hand, I don't know if other reasons may have caused him to go to another country. I can't recall whether his relations with our father were right or not. I knew that he loved and was close to our mother. My mother adored George.

I remember when I saw him leave Smyrna. I was devastated that I had lost my best friend to whom I always looked up too. We got on well, but like brothers, we had our fights sometimes over silly things. I knew that someday that I would see him again. Our sisters were too young to remember him. They only knew him from family photographs. My mother was heartbroken when he left, but our father's position was ambivalent. I shall continue my story with war clouds building up in the Balkans in 1912.

Mihalis Veziris:
The war years 1912-1918

The start of 1912 promised so much but proved a nightmare come October. I was still in school, my sisters were ready to start their education, and our carpet factory continued to do good business.

As war clouds hovered in the distance, I remember the picnics with our family friends at Lake Tantalus where we played without a care in the world. Our world came crashing down when I read that our empire was ready to go to war against our Balkan neighbors. I didn't have a clue nor understood the politics behind this war. I asked my father to explain it to me, but despite his explanation, it was way over my head.

All the daily Smyrna newspapers reported on the progress of the war. Our father kept quiet about the war so as not alienate our Turkish friends. I remember Turkish passions running high against the Christians during the Balkan Wars. Essad Pasha did everything in his power to protect all the citizens of Smyrna from any hostile attacks by the Turkish mobs. His good relations with the leading Greek, Armenian, and Levantine families allowed us to continue living normally against the backdrop of slaughter and mayhem during the war. Our father's relations with Essad proved very good for our family business as well.

When the war finished and treaties signed in late 1913, the Young Turks replaced Essad Pasha with Rahmi Bey. As the new Governor, he immediately sought to cultivate good relations like his predecessor with all the leading families in Smyrna. Rahmi Bey was a cosmopolitan individual who spoke several foreign languages, enjoyed his whiskey, and entertained the wealthy at his villa. Our father always received an invitation from him. This relationship would prove beneficial to later events.

In 1914, I remember the Ottoman government decreed that Turks should boycott all shops owned by Greeks. Rahmi Bey did his utmost to revoke this directive as he wished to protect all foreign businesses, including our own. The political atmosphere in Smyrna was highly charged as relations between Greeks and Turks were on a knife-edge. All it needed was a spark to light the fuse, which would have erupted into violence against the Greeks. Rahmi reduced these tensions by applying a carrot and stick approach.

He published a proclamation in the local press much to the disgust of his masters in Constantinople that if any Turk harmed a Christian or a foreigner, severe punishment would be carried out. On the other hand, his proclamation was well received by the Greeks and other foreign communities in Smyrna. Our local Greek newspapers ran a series of articles praising him for his action. The Young Turks darned not replace him as he was very popular amongst all the citizens of Smyrna.

The big shock came when our empire declared war against Russia in October 1914. I was 14 years old at the time. My sisters Maria and Alexandra were eight and nine years old and didn't understand the consequences of what followed. I remember young Greek and Armenian men rushing off to enlist in the Ottoman army. They wanted to display their patriotism and loyalty to the empire. I was lucky to avoid conscription due to my age and continued my education. Rahmi Bey reassured all citizens that they had nothing fear so long as he remained Governor. Our father was very pleased with Rahmi's announcement. I can say that Rahmi was not your typical Young Turk.

The British blockade of Smyrna didn't impact my family as much as the poorer classes. They faced inflation and high prices that made it difficult for low-income families to meet their daily needs. My family faced difficulties as well but had sufficient funds to ride out the storm of the great war. Our carpet business suffered greatly under the blockade. However, we managed to sell carpets direct to the public at significantly reduced prices. Rahmi continued to purchase his carpets and rugs from us and encouraged his fellow Turks to follow his example.

My father bought a restaurant along the Smyrna quay to supplement our family income. I think he bought it in early 1915 and sold it at the end of the war. It was a smart move where the wealthy elites came to wine and dined. Our region was self-sufficient in foodstuffs, which made it easy to source fresh produce for the restaurant. Sometimes I helped out in the kitchen after school, which would help me in my later life.

There was a shortage of medicine, which made it difficult for doctors to treat patients. Wounded soldiers received top priority over the ordinary citizen regarding treatment. Doctors did remarkable work making medicines last longer than usual. Despite the blockade, the survival rate of the sick and wounded was reasonable. Our newspapers published editorials praising the doctors on their excellent work.

In 1916, I enrolled in the commercial and foreign language school, which was part of the Evangelical School. Here I learned several foreign languages that proved beneficial in communicating with the multilingual population of Smyrna. At times, I felt English and other times, French. It helped me better understand those around me. After all, we lived in a cosmopolitan city with its babble of spoken foreign languages.

I graduated from the school in the middle of 1917. My parents were very proud when I received my diploma being the first to graduate from my siblings. They wanted me to study either medicine or law at Athens University that wasn't possible with war raging in the Balkans. I was never interested in these disciplines but preferred to study history or commerce at Athens University. As far as I know, George found ways to avoid doing his homework. Most times, George would feign illness where our mother would feel sorry for him. George was a trickster and knew how to gain her attention.

Upon graduation, I assisted my father in his businesses until the end of 1919. I learned how he managed them, looked after employees, and interacted with customers. I felt apprehensive at the start, but my confidence increased under his guidance until I could stand on my own two feet. He was an excellent communicator and mentor. The things he taught me greatly helped in my development as a person.

Rahmi Bey received orders from Constantinople to deport Greeks and Armenians into the interior. He disregarded these instructions much to the annoyance of his masters. My father saw Rahmi Bey, who said: " I will protect your family and all the Greeks and Armenians as best I can." There was one instance where he deported a small number of Armenians but returned them to Smyrna within a couple of days. He wanted to show Constantinople that he could be tough when needed. He thumbed his nose at the Young Turks. Rahmi Bey proved to be our friend and protector during the war.

The war ended with our empire accepting the allied armistice terms. My parents and I jumped for joy when we read it in the local press. I know the Turks were angry and upset losing the war, but like us didn't know what the future held for all of us. I hoped that peace would be concluded so life could return to normal. I looked forward to 1919 with high hopes.

Imagining Smyrna, May 15, 1919

I remember the auspicious day of May 15, 1919, when the Greek army landed in Smyrna. It is a day etched in my memory forever, which brought joy to my heart and soul, seeing our Greek army land in the most beautiful city of the Ottoman Empire.

The local Greek newspapers reported on the Paris Peace Conference of rumors that the Greek army might be sent be to Smyrna. I also subscribed to British, French, and American newspapers who offered different perspectives on what was happening in Paris. I received my education at the famous Evangelical school of Smyrna, where I learned foreign languages, which helped me communicate with foreigners and residents of this beautiful city.

I didn't know whether to believe or disbelieve these news stories. Should our Greek brothers arrive in Smyrna, they would be welcomed as our liberators. I am sure many of my fellow Greek Smyrniotes would have shared similar feelings. I was glad we participated on the allied side in the Great War with Eleftherios Venizelos as our great leader. I had no sympathy for King Constantine and his followers, whom I regarded as traitors, who sided with Germany.

We now had an excellent opportunity to realize the Megali Idea. This would bring all our brothers and sisters outside the Hellenic Kingdom into a Megali Ellas. I do recall from newspaper articles that Venizelos put up a brilliant performance delivering our territorial claims before the great powers in Paris. He was an extraordinary politician who brought honor and glory to Greece. Even his enemies conceded that he was a great orator who had captured the imagination of the political leaders and journalists in Paris.

In early May, rumors circulated that a Greek landing at Smyrna would happen very soon based on the decision of Great Britain, France, and the US. The Italians were distrusted and considered rascals trying to upset their allied partners by landing troops in Asia Minor without their consent. I feared that our forces might end up in a spat with our Italian ally in Asia Minor. Such a clash would benefit the Turks who would exploit it for their advantage.

On May 14, the local Greek and foreign-language press revealed that the Greeks were finally coming. When I read this, my heart rejoiced that our day of liberation was at hand after 400 years of Ottoman rule. "They're coming; they're coming," I noted in my private diary. I felt euphoric that I was going to live or experience the most important historical event of my entire life. Smyrna would never be the same again.

The next day, the whole of Smyrna was abuzz with the expectation and excitement that our brothers would finally arrive to liberate us. I walked up to the high ground and had a great view of the entire Bay of Smyrna. I saw Greek navy ships in the distance, moving slowly towards Smyrna harbor. At last, our navy landed with the troops disembarking on the quay, ready to march onto government house (konak).

Our troops arrived on a beautiful warm sunny day. Everyone felt excited about such a momentous occasion. Metropolitan Chrysostomos of Smyrna blessed the troops upon their arrival on the Smyrna quay. Chrysostomos was highly respected by his fellow Smyrniotes, who tended to his flock and maintained good relations with the Ottoman Governor, Rahmi Bey, during the Great War. Rahmi treated us kindly and did everything in his power to protect us from being deported into the Anatolian interior.

On May 15, everyone was well dressed for this special occasion, with all Greek businesses and schools closed on that day. My parents, who owned a small carpet factory, gave all their employees the day off to partake in the celebrations. I will never forget the smile on my parents' faces who had waited for this day with great anticipation.

The streets were thronged with thousands of Greeks waving Greek flags and shouting "Zito o Venizelos," "Zito h Ellas" and "Zito our liberators " as our troops marched towards government house. I, too, was encouraged seeing such a marvelous spectacle. The Turks were most unhappy seeing us giaours (infidels) occupying Smyrna as the former master now became the servant. How times had changed with us firmly ensconced in the saddle.

What followed along the procession to the konak was something that would stain our Greek name and create serious doubts in the minds of our allied friends. As our troops approached, government house shots were fired by unknown individuals, which erupted into chaos and a breakdown of law and order. Our soldiers returned fire to protect themselves. Turkish shops and property were looted and destroyed. According to press reports, some 300 Turks and 100 Greeks were killed with scores of injured victims. The allies in Paris thought they had made the wrong decision to let us go to Smyrna.

Venizelos argued strenuously that we were capable of administering Smyrna on their behalf. He appointed his close friend, Aristidis Sterghiadis, as High Commissioner to govern the city. I was not too fond of Sterghiadis, who showed more considerable sympathy towards the Turks and treated us Smyrniotes with disdain. He was a stern individual who even managed his staff very severely. It was rumored that he hit Smyrniotes with his cane. His relations with Metropolitan Chrysostomos weren't good either. No wonder why we hated him. Whatever one thought of Sterghiadis, he did manage to administer Smyrna with a firm hand.

The allies appointed an inter-allied commission to investigate the events of Smyrna. Many witnesses were interviewed whose testimony did not assist our cause. The inter-allied final report was scathing of our army, whom they considered undisciplined and quick on the trigger in returning fire. Venizelos once again was able to convince the allies that Greece could maintain law and order. Again his oratorical skills and his friendship with British Prime Lloyd George proved to be decisive for Greece.

My brother, George, who arrived in the US in 1908, sponsored me to come here in early 1920. I wrote to George in October 1918, expressing interest in coming to America. He commenced my immigration formalities well before the Greek landing by filing my petition with the US authorities in Washington DC in February 1919. He wrote back to me in early March, telling me to be patient and to wait for a letter for my immigration interview. I received a notification to attend my meeting on July 10, 1919, at the US Consulate in Smyrna.

The Consular official asked me questions about why I wanted to live in America, whether I would be self-supporting if I had relatives already living there, what part of the US I wanted to live, and whether I knew anything about the country. After two hours of questioning, he was satisfied with my answers and stamped my application "APPROVED."

I was confident that everything would go smoothly and was ready to leave for America. Meanwhile, I started to prepare myself for the long trip across the Atlantic bound for New York. I had never travelled on a passenger ship or any kind of ship in my life. I really didn't have any fear of the sea.

I told my parents from the outset that I intended to live in America. At the start, they weren't happy with me but realized that they couldn't stop me. My father and mother gave me their blessing, which meant a lot to me. It symbolized good luck on a journey into the unknown. I had no idea what to expect in my new homeland. I always had the belief that I would do well in America. Where this belief or feeling came from was a mystery for me. I just knew that everything would work out.

I spent the last Christmas with my parents and sisters at our house. On Christmas morning, we all went to St Photini Greek Orthodox Church to hear Chrysostomos deliver his beautiful sermon of what Christ's birth meant for humanity. It was a moving message which brought tears to my eyes, thinking of what laid ahead for me. After the service, we opened up our Christmas presents and enjoyed a beautiful lunch prepared by our Greek cook, Dimitrios. It was a joyous but also a sad occasion knowing that I would be leaving just before the new year

On December 30, 1919, I went to the Smyrna Quay accompanied by my family to board the ship to go to America. My parents were v sad to see me leave, especially my, mother who couldn't hold back her tears. Father was ready to cry but composed himself at the last minute. Maria and Alexandra wore their best dresses to see me off, and both of them told me to write them every week. I promised them that I would that. I said to my parents that we see each other again. Mom and dad were unsure whether we see each other. "Of course, we will," I said.

After an hour, I boarded the ship ready to begin a journey of a lifetime. As the ship slowly left the quay, I waved to my family with mixed feelings of sadness, leaving behind this beautiful metropolis and the joy of starting a new life on the other side of the world.

I couldn't imagine it on December 30, 1919, that I would never see my parents and sisters again. I always lived with the hope that we would be reunited.

Michalis Veziris: I remember 1920

I arrived in America onboard the Greek passenger liner Olympia which docked in New York harbor on January 12, 1920. We were taken to Ellis Island to have our entry papers checked by US Immigration. I also passed the medical with flying colors. " I was ready to go," the doctor said. They found my papers in good order and was now free to enter America. The ferry took us with our worldly possessions to New York from Ellis island. All I had with me was a small suitcase with a few clothes, a pair of shoes and my saved money of US$100.

My brother George, his wife Penelope, and three children were waiting for me. Finally reunited after 12 years, we hugged and embraced each other and cried tears of joy. It was unbelievable, but ultimately, I was now in America. What the future held for me was unknown, but with hard work, I could achieve the same success as my brother, who owned a beautiful restaurant called Bournova in Astoria. He named it Bournova after our place of residence in Smyrna. Despite living America for 12 years, George never forgot his Asia Minor roots.

After a few days of settling into my new surroundings, I needed to work so I could become independent and fulfill my dreams in my new adopted homeland. George employed me as a waiter and dishwasher. The hours were long and paid $10 per week. I enjoyed the work and interacted with all the customers. I learned English in Smyrna, which is a great blessing in America, allowing you to strike a conversation with people. I came across some Americans who called me a " Greek dog," a "Turk," and told me to return to my old country. Such epithets remind me of being called a giaour by the Turks in Smyrna. I did my best to ignore such people and focus on becoming successful in America.

As 1920 rolled on, I wrote letters to my parents and siblings back in Smyrna, telling them about my experience living in America. The letters were the only way I could communicate with my family in Smyrna. I mentioned that I was grateful for George providing me with work and accommodation until such time that I could stand on my own two feet. My parents told me that the economic and political conditions in Smyrna were perfect under the Greek administration. Father said in one of his letters that his business was booming. I was so pleased to hear such positive news.

In one letter, my father stated that he was exporting some of his carpets and rugs to the United States. One day passing by a furniture and carpet store, I saw our carpets and rugs on display sold at a reasonable price. I went inside the store, and one of the sales staff approached me to ask whether I wished to purchase a carpet. I mentioned to him that my father produced them. The salesman told me that the customers were delighted to pay a little bit more for such quality merchandise. My father was happy to receive such positive feedback.

Maria and Alexandra were always happy to receive my letters. I kept my promise to write to them. Both of them were doing well in school, but they missed my presence. In one of their letters, Alexandra described playing the role of the teacher with Maria acting as the student. Alexandra pretended to be a Greek language teacher with Maria, the keen student willing to learn. They often switched roles playing teacher/student. I always felt that my sisters would become good school teachers.

In-between work and some leisure time, I followed the political developments unfolding in Greece through articles in the National Herald (Venizelist) and Atlantis (Royalist) newspapers, which represented the different Greek political factions on American soil. The Atlantis is rabidly anti-Venizelist, which criticizes Venizelos and the liberal party at every opportunity. As far as it is concerned, Venizelos's policies are bad for Greece and are leading the nation down the path to destruction. King Constantine is their hero who can do no wrong.

On the other hand, the National Herald supports the policies of Venizelos to the hilt. It argues that Greece, under Venizelos, has the support of two major powers: Great Britain and France, and also achieved its territorial expansion under the Treaty of Sevres. Venizelos is a national hero who united the country during the recent World War.

However, a disturbing event happened in October, when I read about young King Alexander fighting for his life. A pet monkey bit him on the palace grounds of Tatoi just outside Athens, which resulted in a political crisis in Greece. While I am no royalist, I like King Alexander, who is very popular with the vast majority of mainland Greeks and my compatriots in Smyrna. His popularity rests with his ability to work closely with Venizelos on domestic and foreign policy issues.

When news of Alexander's death reached America, Venizelos called a general election for early November to allow the Greek people to vote for a new Voule. The Royalists were actively involved with their propaganda campaign both in America and Greece, denouncing Venizelos as a dictator. I believed that the Liberal party would win the election in a landslide. Even the American press believed in a Venizelist victory.

When I read of Venizelos's election defeat, I felt shocked, horror, numb, unbelievable with the Royalists winning a massive majority in the new Voule and calling for a referendum for the return of King Constantine. I am upset with the idea of Constantine returning to Athens, who, as an individual, betrayed us in surrendering Fort Rupel in Eastern Macedonia to a German-Bulgarian force during the Great War. Constantine's so-called benevolent neutrality was a sham.

I believe that the referendum should have never taken place. The Royalists in America are ecstatic with their election success in Greece and the return of Constantine from exile. I have some royalist friends here who have told me that Constantine will bring honor and glory for Greece. I'm afraid I have to disagree with their views but remain friends with them. Some are neighbors and customers. Sometimes Venizelist and Royalist disagreements in America have resulted in fights with police called in to cool down tempers. It gives us Greeks a bad name in America. It's a shame that we can debate our differences in a civilized manner.

The sad thing about the final result in the Greek election is the abandonment of Greece by its allied partners: Britain, France, and Italy. The British and French distrust Constantine for his conduct during the Great War. I feel the withdrawal of support from our allied partners would be a curse for Greece. I fear for the future of our people in Asia Minor with the allies talking about modifying the Treaty of Sevres and making concessions to the Kemalists. It is unclear whether Constantine will continue with Venizelos's foreign policy or withdraw our army from Asia Minor.

With Constantine returning to Athens, he gave reassurance to the allies that the Greek army would remain in Asia Minor. My heart is at peace once again of reading Constantine's positive statement. We don't want to lose or give up our territorial gains for fighting alongside our allies in the last world war.

It was essential to maintain Venizelos's legacy at all costs. Our soldiers didn't die in vain in the great war.

Mihalis Veziris: 1921 a year of ups and downs in America

It is the start of 1921, and I am looking forward to this year with much anticipation. I have been here for nearly two years and continue to work at my brother's restaurant in Astoria, and business is booming. My brother George is thinking of making me a partner in his restaurant. It would be an honor to work alongside him as we get on very well together.

More and more Americans are coming to try our Greek cuisine, which they find delicious and sometimes ask us for recipes of how to make baklava, dolmades, and mousaka. I tell them they are secret family recipes from the old country. They are surprised at my response. Our Greek customers tell me our dishes remind them of the old country.

The local Greek newspapers gave our restaurant a wonderful review telling readers that we offered an excellent menu at reasonable prices. My brother believed that if you charged too much, that would drive business away. Our prices were meager compared to other Greek restaurants in New York. The newspaper review helped us to attract new customers.

On weekends, we have a local Greek band which plays the latest songs from Greece and Asia Minor. The rebetika songs of Smyrna bring tears to my eyes, taking me back to another time, remembering my family when I lived there. Greek dancing is very popular with our customers. The breaking of plates is something our American customers find unusual. One American customer who has his own business is willing to sell us plates at a reduced price, which I think is funny. Yep! We did take him up on his offer.

Life in America can be tough but rewarding if you work hard. My finances are improving and have been able to save money. I have a little leisure time. I send money regularly to my folks in Smyrna, not that they need it. Father's carpet factory is booming as he exports most of his stuff to Greece and America. The money I send is set aside as a dowry for my sisters' future weddings. Maria and Alexandra are 14 and 15 years old. I suppose in a couple of years, and they will marry into some wealthy Greek family in Smyrna. I will do my best to attend their weddings.

As my savings increase, I am facing the problem of whether to buy my own house or not. It is achievable as house prices in Astoria are affordable. Our home in Smyrna would be considered a palace here. I remember it with its exquisite gardens, manicured lawns, and the gardeners my father employs to maintain such a stately home. We had servants to do the cooking, cleaning, and shopping for us. I do miss life in Smyrna with its many beautiful Greek cafes, stores, clubs, and theaters. These are beautiful memories to have brought over in my new, adopted homeland.

I keep an eye on political developments in Greece and Smyrna through the press. I receive Greek newspapers from Smyrna, which my folks regularly send me. The return of King Constantine and his government concerned me for the future of our compatriots in Smyrna. My concern would be borne out with the London Conference to discuss modifications to the Treaty of Sevres. I understand inviting the Sultan's delegation as it is the official government of the Ottoman Empire, but to ask the rebel Kemalists to the peace table is disgusting. The Sultan considered Mustapha Kemal a traitor and a rebel from what I read in the press.

The Turks were eager to accept modifications to the peace treaty. Still, our side regarded it as a legal document under international law whose provisions should be enforced by military means. Our allied friends ignored our case, who were more interested in coming to terms with Kemal.

During July-August, the Greek army began its inland march into Anatolia with the prime objective of defeating Kemal and occupying his capital, Angora (Ankara). I read with excitement in the press of our army's series of impressive military victories at Afion Karahissar and Eskisehir. Angora, here we come ready to deliver the mortal blow to the Kemalist regime once and for all.

Imagine for a moment what would have happened if we had occupied Angora. There would have been celebrations and rejoicings from Greek communities all over the world. I am sure such an event would have raised Constantine's reputation in the eyes of the Venizelists. Church bells would ring loudly with the clergy blessing our troops. The Gordian knot would be cut, and Asia Minor would be ours.

I was surprised to read of the fierce resistance the Turks put up to defend their capital. There were moments when our army overwhelmed them with Angora ready to fall into our hands. However, the Turks counter-attacked and pushed us back to the Afion Karahissar-Eskishehr defensive line, which in my mind would be the death knell for our compatriots in Asia Minor. I didn't realize at the time that my statement would turn out to be prophetic.

The French signed a treaty with the Kemalists, which sidelined the Sultan and legitimized Kemal's regime in Angora. Our British friends were most displeased with this French action, which created tensions between London and Paris. Oh! Those Frenchies what horrible double-dealers they were. They plunged their knife into us in Asia Minor. I am angry with the French over this.

While the future of our compatriots seemed uncertain in Asia Minor, my parents, in their letters, kept reassuring me that our army is protecting them from the Kemalists despite the military deadlock. Smyrniotes went about their daily lives without a care in the world.

Stores were full of the latest ladies' fashion from Paris, and the Smyrna Opera House staged terrific concerts. Life was reasonable under the Greek administration.

Looking from afar, I guess we were at a military disadvantage as the Turks could take their time and attack us at their convenience. When that would happen would not bode well for our fellow compatriots.

With the darkening clouds circling over Asia Minor, a ray of sunshine came in the shape of our national hero, Eleftherios Venizelos, visiting America. The US press was full of praise for this great man who was welcomed by local Greek communities wherever he visited. Of course, that Atlantis was displeased with Venizelos being here. They hated him with a passion, which made me sick. On the other hand, the National Herald was honored to have our national hero among us. If only this man could return to power in Greece. Maybe our allied friends might swing back in supporting us instead of Kemal. The possibility of that happening was difficult to state as the circumstances had drastically changed in 1921 compared to 1919-20.

Anyway, 1921 ended on a happy note with Venizelos's visit to America. So many of our Greeks in America were ecstatic to see this great man in the flesh.

1922: A year to forget

Another new year full of high hopes and resolutions for success. My brother George decided to reduce his time in the restaurant due to health reasons. He asked me to assume responsibility for running it. I considered a challenge that I would do my best to live up to his expectations. George was a perfectionist, no short cuts with him, and took great pride in the food served to our customers. No wonder why they kept coming back for more.

The business was so good that the premises we rented were too small for our current needs. We previously discussed in late 1921 to find larger premises somewhere in Astoria. After several months, we found the ideal location to expand our business. Most of the existing customers were happy with our choice of location who continued to support us and also attracted new clientele. There was more room for the band to play compared to the cramped space of our previous establishment.

I still lived with my brother and his family and decided against buying my own house at this time. Running the business left me very little time for anything else. I remained a bachelor and hadn't found the right woman of my dreams as yet. Some of my local Greek friends tried to arrange a marriage to women in their families.

Sometimes a party was organized with a specific purpose for me to meet their sister. I always managed to sidestep such an event. I know they meant well, but I wasn't interested in marriage at this stage. Hopefully, some lady would capture my heart in the future.

I continued corresponding with the folks in Smyrna. They reassured me that everything was fine and had nothing to fear from the Turks. I don't know whether my parents didn't want to worry me about the real situation evolving in Asia Minor. I suspected from the press reports that something big was brewing. My instincts proved me right and felt uneasy about the army's presence in Anatolia. Their failure to defeat Kemal would hurt us big time later in 1922.

Our so-called allied friends convened a conference in Paris to resolve the Greek-Turkish conflict. They gave the Kemalists what they wanted, meaning that our army would need to withdraw from Asia Minor. A truce arrangement to ensure the belligerents would execute the Allied conditions.

Athens sought to withdraw from Asia Minor as its finances were in a parlous state. With no credit coming from our allies, we could no longer prosecute the war to its logical conclusion. The main issue that troubled me what was to become of our compatriots and other minorities left behind after our troop withdrawal. I felt that Athens had betrayed us. The Kemalist task of winning the war had become so much easier for them, and of course, I knew what awaited the Greeks and Armenians in the end.

In May, I read press reports of our two American relief workers Dr. Mark Ward and Frank Yowell, who told the world of the deportation of men, women, and children from the Black sea towns and villages into the Anatolian interior. As witnesses to these horrors, they reported it to the allied authorities in Constantinople. An international commission of inquiry was to be formed to investigate their claims of massacres. However, French procrastination was intended to delay the investigation, which never eventuated. Our French and Italian allies were pro-Kemalist to the bone. I hated the French more and more with each passing day. For some strange reason, I didn't feel hateful towards the Italians. I greatly admired the British prime minister, Lloyd George, who supported us in Asia Minor.

Out of the blue, Athens threatened to occupy Constantinople in late July to force the Kemalists to the peace table. However, the British threatened to shell Piraeus forcing Athens to back down quickly. I was surprised at the British decision, which I found puzzling and thinking that they would have been happy seeing us ending the war. I can only assume that Lloyd George was outflanked by the conservative members of his cabinet who supported Turkey. Our threats were toothless — what a joke of a regime.

It seemed to me that our Greek government was on its last legs. How true that proved to be when the Kemalists attacked our positions on a broad front in Asia Minor. Our army morale had collapsed and now began a hurried withdrawal to Smyrna, with thousands of refugees following behind to avoid Turkish reprisals. Smyrna would become a city full of Greeks seeking to escape from the man-made hell to come.

I was concerned about the future of my parents and siblings in Smyrna. When the Kemalists entered the city, I thought maybe law and order would prevail, and the Turks would protect the lives and properties of the Greeks. How wrong I was.

When I read about the burning of Smyrna by the Turks, I cried bitter tears remembering this once beautiful city being reduced to an ash heap and not knowing the fate of my family. I wrote letters to my Congressman, State Department, and President Harding asking them to find out what happened to them. I received unsatisfactory replies from them, which much disappointed me. I felt they wanted to sweep this matter aside and weren't interested in the fate of our compatriots who remained or had perished in Asia Minor.

While the restaurant was doing well, I couldn't sleep, I had nightmares and my nerves were on edge not knowing the fate of my family. I would snap at anyone who spoke to me. I couldn't continue my life like this. I was a nervous wreck like so many of our local Greek compatriots who had relatives in Smyrna.

I contacted the American Red Cross and Near East Relief offices in New York, who made every effort to trace them. According to their investigations, my entire family had either perished in the Smyrna fire or had been deported into the Anatolian interior by the Turks. At least, they provided an answer but had a massive heart feeling that I would never see them again.

George never said much about our parents and kept most things to himself. I don't know whether he had personal differences with them and never corresponded with them since he arrived in America. It is like George completely severed his links with Smyrna. He refused to discuss it with me. I kept all my parents' letters as a reminder of their existence in Smyrna. My beautiful Smyrna will remain forever etched in my heart.

The one thing that pleased me was the abdication of Constantine and the execution of the Royalist politicians, including military officers. They deserved what they got. The Atlantis newspaper was saddened with Constantine's departure and the execution of the Royalist ministers. It was a travesty of justice for them and heaped all the blame for the Asia Minor disaster on Venizelos. They forgot it was their lot who lost who us Asia Minor.

The National Herald considered Constantine and his ministers a blight on Greek politics. Good riddance was the tone in the articles of this newspaper. I hoped that our grand champion Venizelos would lead Greece once again. That never happened at this time.

Our Smyrniot compatriots were refugees in mainland Greece and the Greek islands. They needed help, and without our American relief agencies, many of them would have perished from hunger, disease, lack of shelter, and cold weather. When President Harding announced a public appeal to raise funds to help the refugees, I sent $200 as my contribution. The American public contributed generously to this appeal.

Yes! 1922 was a year to forget which left painful memories that could never be erased.

Mihalis Veziris doing well in America: 1923

My brother George told me that he could no longer continue his interest in the restaurant. His health was failing and didn't know how long he had to live. "You will now run the business on your own," George told me. "What about Penelope and your children," I said. "Don't worry, Penelope is not interested in the business; she's interested in taking care of the children: Alexander, Amelia, and Vasili," said George. All this time, George never told me his medical condition. I didn't understand his attitude about why he didn't want to share his pain with me.

Imagine after three years, and I would be running my own business in America in such a short space of time. Indeed, this is a beautiful country where opportunities abound. My mission was now to build up the business further. I had a vision of owning several restaurants. I felt positive about the future, but George's illness was always at the back of my mind. It's good to dream big in America.

Besides business, I follow in the events of Asia Minor, and I kept thinking of my family who could have perished in the Smyrna fire or deported into the Anatolian interior. The latter one worried me thinking that my parents could have ended up working on those infamous labor battalions. That was like signing their death sentence. My sisters were attractive girls and could have ended up in some Turkish harem. I hope that wasn't the case.

Our great Venizelos was to represent us at Lausanne. Our allied friends had their agendas to settle with the Turks. I was interested in the fate of our compatriots. This great man would use his diplomatic skills to salvage what he could for Greece. It was not an easy task facing a resurgent Turkey who turned its defeat in the great war into a great military and diplomatic victory.

Two issues still buzzed around in my head since September 1922. I remember reading about the terrible death that our beloved Archbishop Chrysostomos suffered at the hands of the Turkish mob. This man was a saint who did everything to protect his flock from the Turks. He was proud of his Greek heritage. I remember as a young man attending one of his church sermons. Wow! his message was so powerful that it still touches my soul today. He didn't deserve the horrible torture and humiliation, which ended his life. A saint, if ever there was one.

The other event was the Smyrna fire firmly etched in my mind. I remember seeing the large banner headlines in the American and Greek press about the destruction of this magnificent city of the Near East. In my view, it was the jewel in the crown of the Ottoman Empire. What a city that was alive with business, culture, trade, and entertainment activity. According to the press, it was the Turks who burned the European, Greek, and Armenian quarters of Smyrna.

The fire destroyed many foreign businesses, including my father's carpet factory. I wondered whether the insurance would cover our losses. Imagine that all hard work going up in smoke. We received no compensation for our losses, which made me feel very sad.

I always had a faint hope that my family might have survived. Throughout 1923, I continued making inquiries with our relief organizations to ascertain the fate of my family. I don't know how many times I visited the offices of the Red Cross and Near East Relief to receive the latest updates. Finally, the American Red Cross told me that they perished in the fire according to the information which they received. I burst out into tears when they told me the news of their deaths. At last, there was closure knowing of their tragic end, but not seeing them again proved even more distressful. There was nothing I could do about it but to accept it with a heavy heart.

My sister-in-law, Penelope, decided to move her family to the warmer climes of southern California. I later learned that she had relatives in Los Angeles. I saw them off at the Grand railway station for the last time. I was very sad to them leave as they had treated me so kindly. Before boarding the train, Penelope told me that George had died of an incurable disease and could no longer live in New York. Penelope sold me her family home and had enough money to live comfortably on the west coast.

The newspapers reported at the Lausanne conference. Imagine, the once defeated Turks came back as victors dictating their terms to the allies. I was outraged over this but could do nothing about it. Even if I wrote a protest letter to my local Congressman, he would refer it to the State Department.

Venizelos had the difficult task of negotiating with the victorious Turks. He used his oratory skills to salvage what he could for Greece. The Turks insisted on the removal of the Patriarchate from Constantinople, but fortunately, the British and French supported our position of non-removal. Venizelos did not budge an inch on the future of the Patriarchate. Luckily, the Turks backed down in the end.

The Turks were very obstinate during the conference egged on by the French. The French were two-faced, supporting you on the one hand and stabbing you in the back on the other. Horrible creatures, the French. At least the British supported us as they didn't like the Turks. They, too, had their agenda, the oil fields of Mosul. America was an observer and didn't contribute much to the conference.

The refugee crisis was a significant issue for Greece. Our old homeland lacked the economic and financial resources to cope with this humanitarian crisis. As I wrote in a previous diary entry, our American relief agencies have been magnificent in providing aid to our poor compatriots. I also thank our American public for its generosity.

I am to call myself an American, even though I still had two years to go before I could become a citizen of this great country. When I finally received my naturalization papers, my heart was at peace. Wow! Holding an American passport was like wearing a badge of honor.

In early May, there were rumblings of war between the Turks and us. The press reported that Ismet Pasha wanted war reparations from Greece, but Venizelos told him, " we don't have the money to pay you. Look at our refugee crisis." Ismet insisted on payment, but we threatened Angora with military action. They backed down in the end. No one wanted war. I am glad common sense prevailed.

Finally, the peace treaty was signed between us and Turkey and hopefully no more wars in the Near East. That area has suffered so much, with millions of people killed or forced to flee to nearby countries. I hope my Asia Minor compatriots will have the opportunity to rebuild their lives in Greece. Of course, it won't be easy, but they are resourceful people to achieve success in their "new" country.

I was happy that our American government would allow some of our Greek refugees to resettle here before the new immigration rules that would come into force in 1924. I believe some of them were sponsored by relatives already living in the US.

Penelope wrote, saying that she was glad of her move to Los Angeles, where she bought a beautiful house with a garden. Her children loved it also and no longer needed to shovel snow. New York was very cold in winter.

It is great that Penelope has found peace in Los Angeles since George's death. She wanted to get as far away from New York as possible as it evoked terrible memories for her. We corresponded for a few years, exchanging stories of how her children were doing in school and how her family had adjusted to life in Los Angeles.

So 1923 ended on a good note and looked forward to 1924 and beyond.

Mihalis Veziris: the final chapter

With the Asia Minor issue resolved, 1924 was my 4th year in America. I experienced so much emotional pain over the past 15 months, losing my entire family in the Smyrna fire and the death of my brother, George. Dispute the difficulties; life must continue.

Over the next few years, our restaurant boomed and found me in the fortunate position of buying two more restaurants in downtown New York. The money was flowing in like rivers of gold. They call America the land of dreams. Anything is possible if you prepared to work for it.

I employed 70 staff in my three restaurants who came from various ethnic backgrounds: Italians, Armenians, French, Greeks, and Americans. Some of them had limited knowledge of English and were able to speak to them in their native tongue. I learned French, Italian, and some Armenian when I attended the famous Evangelical School in Smyrna.

I took a keen interest in my employees' welfare and their families and also paid them good wages. My office door was always open for them to come and discuss their concerns with me. My employees were enthusiastic about the job, treated the customers with courtesy and respect, and always had a smile on their faces. A happy look ensured more business.

I decided to take my first trip to Greece in March 1929. I wanted to visit the Parthenon and the ancient sites around Athens. I was also curious to see how our Asia Minor refugees had settled into their new environment. I had three good managers to look after things during my absence. They ran my businesses like as if they owned them. I was proud of Kostas, Dimitrios and Gus for the sterling work they did for me. Of course, Gus was another name for Constantine in America. How the name Constantine became Gus was mystery for me.

I sailed from New York on March 12, 1929, onboard the SS Alexander for Piraeus via Marseilles, France. It took eight days to cross the Atlantic. We experienced terrible weather with strong winds and high seas. I thought our ship would sink to the bottom of the Atlantic with its entire crew and passengers. The weather in the Mediterranean was delightful with calm seas compared to the Atlantic.

I finally arrived in Piraeus on March 20 and told the taxi driver to take me to the Hotel Bretagne in Athens. This hotel would be my central point during my stay in Athens. I visited the Parthenon, perched on top of a hill overlooking Athens. I imagined myself transported back to the time of Pericles, watching him address the Athenian assembly. The one thing that struck me about Athens was the construction of new neighborhoods, factories, and roads to accommodate its expanding population resulting from the Asia Minor disaster. The refugees were hardworking, diligent, and eager to do well in Greece. They could never return to their ancestral homeland because of the exchange of population agreement between us and Turkey.

Many carpet factories were established in Attiki, produced beautiful carpets and rugs which were exported overseas. These factories were profitable due to the availability of cheap local labor. Wages were low, making it difficult for families to meet their daily expenses. If you worked fulltime, that helped to some extent but employed as a casual was terrible, for the latter work was irregular.

One day I ran into some Smyrniotes in Nea Smyrni who remembered me. They were so happy to see me after all those years living in America. A few of them remembered my parents with a fondness that brought tears to my eyes. Stefanos Manos and Christos Papadoukas were close friends of my father. Both of them had been involved in the import/export business in Smyrna. They invited me to their houses for dinner, and we shared memories of a bygone era. They recounted the beautiful days living in Smyrna, enjoying comfortable and luxurious social lives. Manos told me that some of his neighbors had owned businesses, farms, and others were doctors, lawyers, bankers, merchants, and accountants. The Smyrna fire was something that many of them did not wish to discuss with me. Painful memories for them where they had lost everything. They have never received compensation for the destruction of their properties.

Before going to Salonika, I visited Mt Olympus, the home of the Greek Gods and Olympia, the site of the ancient Olympic Games. I imagined myself participating in the ancient games and winning the 1500 meters race. These two places are magical, taking one back to another time and place. I thought Zeus would send one of his thunderbolts down from Mt Olympus. I always wondered how our ancient ancestors could have believed and worshipped twelve Gods instead of one God. Religion was a central element in the lives of our ancient Greeks.

I spent a couple of months in Salonika and also took the opportunity to visit some of the towns and villages in Macedonia and Western Thrace. To my surprise, I found new agricultural settlements and tobacco planters from Pontus settled in the Kavalla region. The refugees had increased agrarian production, repaired disused houses left behind by the Turks and Bulgarians, and constructed new dwellings in the northern areas of Greece. Salonika, like Athens, had experienced a massive influx of refugees from Asia Minor too. In my opinion, refugees living in rural communities fared better than those in large towns and cities.

I visited Crete to learn more about Venizelos. The Cretans told me he was their national hero and hung pictures of him in their houses.

His fellow Cretans called him our Lefterakis. I am proud to call myself a Venizelist. Of course, Venizelos was in power, doing an excellent job for Greece. This remarkable Greek political figure commanded the respect of the international community. However, his enemies still lurked in the shadows.

I decided on the spur of the moment to visit Smyrna to see what it looked like after the 1922 fire. I stayed there for a week entering Turkey on my American passport. Smyrna had suffered significant damage during the earthquake of April 1928. The Turks were doing their utmost to repair the damage to their city. I walked along the quay, trying to imagine the suffering of our people during those black days of September 1922. My family must have suffered a terrible death in that ordeal.

The stock market crash on Wall Street in October 1929 hastened my return to America. Upon my arrival in late December, I had to evaluate my business viability. I closed two of my restaurants and fired staff whom I could no longer afford to employ. It was the hardest decision I ever made letting go of such a loyal and dedicated team. My decision impacted their families, as well. My choice was either survival or shut down.

I kept our original restaurant in Astoria open with 15 employees, reducing prices and cutting wages to remain afloat. People didn't have enough money to purchase the bare essentials of life. Some homeless people came looking to do any work or asked for any leftover food. Employment was out of the question, but we did provide free food to the homeless. That was the least I could do.

I survived this difficult economic time, and business started picking up just before the start of World War 2. I read press reports of the heroism displayed by the Greek army, which nearly drove the Italians into the Ionian Sea. Of course, Ioannis Metaxas's historic OXI

(NO) to Mussolini showed us that our compatriots were ready and willing to defend the patrida to the last soldier. Our fellow Cretans did everything to repel the German invasion of their island but succumbed to a superior force in the end. Our Greek American Relief organization (GRA) raised funds to be sent via the Red Cross to assist our Greek brethren under German occupation. I sent $500 towards their appeal. On several occasions, I organized special dinners at our restaurant with the money collected, going to the GRA.

After the war, my economic position improved once again, making lots of money. I bought another restaurant near Times Square, which proved a financial bonanza. Its location was perfect, with so many passing customers stopping off for lunch and dinner. We offered the same menu as the one in our Astoria restaurant. Both businesses were lucrative, which allowed me to enjoy a lifestyle before my imagination. After 40 years, I sold them all and retired to Miami, Florida, in 1960.

Overall, America has been kind to me and allowed me to become a successful businessman. I survived the economic depression of the 1930s and rebuilt my financial and economic fortune. The enormous pain of all was losing my parents in 1922 and never got the chance to say a final goodbye.

CHAPTER 2

MELINA'S STORY: A WOMAN SURVIVOR FROM PONTUS

I am an Asia Minor refugee named Melina Panayotides from the Black Sea city of Trebizond. When the Kemalists won the war, the Turkish soldiers started to round us up and took us to transit camps close to the Asia Minor coast to be sent to Greece.

We marched from Trebizond down Adana near the Mediterranean coast. Along the way, we walked in long convoys of men, women, and children passing through high snow- capped mountains, crossing wide rivers and deserts, and finally arriving in Adana.

Our captors never told us what our final destination would be but to be ready to leave at short notice. We were told to take very few personal things with us. All kinds of dark thoughts entered my mind. I even contemplated suicide for a short time. That was not a solution. I thought of the future of my two children, Ioannis and Maria, aged five and six, respectively. I didn't want them to be orphans.

As we proceeded, the older men and women perished from hunger, ill-treatment, disease, and starvation. The Turks moved us at breakneck speed to arrive in Adana. I didn't realize that Adana was some fifty miles from the coast. These poor old souls couldn't keep up with us younger ones. They were simply left to die on the side of dusty and muddy roads without a proper burial. Of course, the wild animals devoured their carcasses, leaving no trace of their human existence. It was a terrible way to die without paying our last respects to these elderly folks.

The Turkish soldiers took our young men to secluded spots and executed them. Their bodies were thrown down ravines and stuffed into empty caves. Many of the young women were carried off by soldiers and irregulars to harems. Some women converted to Islam to save their lives. Other women preferred death to conversion. I was left alone by the Turks. I cannot understand why they left me alone, even though I considered myself to be attractive. Maybe my prayers were protecting us from the evil surrounding us.

I had my two young children with me. Our food rations consisted of little black bread, some bean soup, and water, which were insufficient to feed us all. I divided our rations as best I could to ensure the children received the best "portions" under such cruel circumstances. Sometimes I was fortunate to find and hide morsels of food such as bread to give the children without being seen by the Turkish soldiers. If I got caught, I risked being rifle butted, kicked, and even shot.

The only thing that kept us going was the will to live. Despite our trials and tribulations, my faith and daily prayers to the Virgin Mary sustained us through this very excruciating time. It's a time that should never be forgotten and to record such painful memories for posterity.

There were nights when I remembered the beautiful life I enjoyed with my husband, Constantine, in Trebizond. We were not rich but lived a comfortable life making our living from a small business we owned on the outskirts of the city. We sold both local and imported foodstuffs, clothes, cigarettes, and tobacco products. Most of our merchandise was purchased locally from Greek and Armenian wholesalers.

I was educated at the local Greek gymnasium for girls in Trebizond. We were required to wear a school uniform. Our hair had to be curled, attended church every Sunday, and had to behave like ladies before everyone. Our education was similar to that taught to boys in Greece. I studied religion, Greek, mathematics, physics, history, and French. Besides these subjects, I studied sewing, carpeting, embroidery, and cooking. The education I received prepared me to take my place as a wife and a homemaker.

I assisted Constantine when he got swamped in the business. It allowed me to interact with other women where our conversations centered on our families and got me out of the kitchen. In my spare time, I mended clothes for my Greek and Turkish neighbors and friends. The extra income helped our business and family life. We had no servants like some of the wealthy families in Trebizond. Some names of the wealthy families included: Papadopoulos, Phillipidis, and Xenidis (Greek), Papazian, Alexandrian, and Mochanian (Armenian) and Ahmet Pasha, Edhem Bey and Fevzi Effendi (Turks).

Constantine was a tall, proud man with a black mustache who treated us well. He was a good father and always found time to play with the children. Our customers liked him as a person, including our Turkish friends. Surprisingly, we got on very well with them. They considered him an honest, kind, and honorable man who treated them with respect. He always took the time to listen to their concerns and sometimes offered advice.

In May 1920, Constantine traveled to Smyrna to enlist in the Greek army. He was carried away by the sweeping victories of our

Greek army. Even though he never visited Greece, he was very proud of his Greek heritage. He wrote many letters from the war front detailing his experience fighting the Turks. The military censor censored some of his messages for security reasons.

In some of his last letters, he described the military success of our army in capturing Afion Karahissar and Eskisehir. His biggest dream was the prized occupation of Ankara. Before his death just outside Ankara, he believed our military would cut the Gordian knot in Asia Minor. His vision of defeating Mustapha Kemal never materialized. We lost the war and never cut the Gordian knot. The Greek War ministry sent me a telegram, which took about a week to arrive at my home via the Spanish Consul in Trebizond. It stated that Constantine died a hero's death for the motherland. I was devastated when I learned of his death but believed his contribution served a higher good.

I was surprised when some of our Turkish neighbors were very sad to hear of Constantine's death. They held in high esteem and liked him as a person. Such comforting at a difficult time helped me to better cope with a painful situation. Of course, there were Turks who regarded him as a traitor to the Ottoman homeland and deserved to die. There were some Turks who detested Mustapha Kemal considering a traitor to the Sultan, whereas the vast majority of Turks were pro-Kemalist. People say that war brings out the animal instincts in us humans.

In the last months of the war, the Kemalists deported many of our friends and relatives from Trebizond and surrounding villages into the Anatolian desert. Many of them did not survive their ordeal. For reasons I can't explain, call it fate or luck, I was not deported and continued to run our business unmolested until the order came for us to leave.

It must have been late November or early December 1922, when we arrived in Adana. We were tired, looked emaciated, our clothes had become rags, but spirits never wavered. We believed we would make it and that we did. We survived to tell our story.

We waited in the camp to be picked up by American and British ships. The camp conditions were atrocious. There was overcrowding squeezed in like sardines, with little or no sanitation, given meager rations, diseases were rife with very little medical care. Death was the victor.

The Turks treated us very poorly and were beaming from ear-to-ear when the foreign ships finally came to remove us from Mersina. We marched from Adana to Mersina over terrible dusty and muddy roads . Turkish women and children verbally abused us and threw stones at us. Angry Turks hit us with sticks and spat at us.

I will continue my story another time about my experience living in a refugee camp in Greece.

A journey from Mersina to Piraeus: a woman's ship experience

I waited nearly five months before an American freighter whose name I can't remember took us to Greece. We walked some fifty miles from Adana along dusty unmade roads to the port of Mersina on the southeast coast of Turkey. Waiting for our rescue ship seemed like an eternity. Time moved so slowly that kept asking myself, "when is this darn ship going to come to take us?." When it finally arrived, the Turks moved us quickly from the transit camp onto the quay to get rid of us.

We were herded like cattle on the two decks of the ship. I thought sardines had more room and a better chance of survival than us. The vessel departed from Mersina with its human cargo of 2000 lost souls. I was in a daze, a fog surrounded me, a lost soul with an uncertain future. Sadness was also etched on the faces of my children Ioannis and Maria. I befriended a couple of families around me to pass the time. We exchanged stories of our homeland and families, which were full of beautiful memories.

I had no idea what awaited my children in the land of our Greek ancestors and me. I felt I was coming back home after an absence of nearly 3000 years. It was a strange feeling. I wondered whether we would be welcomed home or not. I didn't know that our compatriot refugees who had arrived in Greece earlier were poorly treated by the locals. These were called horrible names, which I won't repeat and were told to go back from whence they came from.

The ship's captain and his officers did their best to make our journey as comfortable as possible. Feeling comfortable was an understatement. We had no cover putting up with rain, hot sun, and strong winds. The nights were freezing. The children and I huddled close to each other to keep warm. Other families did the same as us. We were lucky we didn't catch pneumonia from exposure to the elements.

Food was scarce and had to make it last as long as possible. I divided the food with the children receiving more substantial portions than myself. The diet consisted of dried bread, some fruit, and water. At least the Americans gave us more to eat than our Turkish captors. We were lucky to have these wonderful Americans taking care of us. They showed us why Americans were admired and respected by everyone in Asia Minor.

The American sailors entertained us with their music playing their banjos, guitars, and harmonicas. They sang popular American songs which helped us momentarily to forget our woes. It was a pleasant diversion. Some of our compatriots wanted to dance, but there wasn't enough space. There was a Greek-American sailor who was a blessing for all of us. He acted as our interpreter, conveying our concerns to the ship's captain.

Sickness and disease were rife onboard our ship unhelped by the unsanitary conditions with so many people huddled so close together. Cholera, typhus, and smallpox cut like a knife resulting in many deaths. Our compatriots were buried at sea. They never got a chance to at least see their ancestral homeland.

We had three doctors who worked tirelessly almost to the point of collapsing from sheer exhaustion tending to the medical needs of their compatriots. The ship's doctor helped out whenever he was needed to relieve our overworked doctors. Having little or no medication made their task even more difficult in treating their patients. They soldiered on as best they could to keep the sick ones alive as long as possible. Many gave up the ghost. I don't remember how many died but think it was around 20% of our compatriots.

We traveled two days before the ship stopped off at one of the islands. Some of our compatriots requested to be dropped off at our first port of call. The vessel berthed at Karpathos at 6 AM. Greek officials refused to take them. The island was overflowing with a mass of people against a background of white tents, which I viewed from the ship's deck. I guessed there may have been up to ten thousand plus refugees. I wondered from other parts of Asia Minor our compatriot refugees came from.

I couldn't believe seeing so many people confined to such small area stretching from near the harbor up to the top of the surrounding hills. I imagined an artist had painted his canvas white, which only required to fill in human faces showing sadness, anguish, and destitution etched on the refugees' faces. I immediately thought their fate would become mine as well. I thought correctly.

At Karpathos, we stayed about half a day before boarding the boat, hopefully onto our final destination, Piraeus. We were only allowed to walk along the quay. Greek officials made sure to restrict us to a particular confined area. My children became agitated and restless, so I had thought of something to keep them entertained and quiet. I told them children's stories, which quietened down and made them feel a bit happier. The businesses along the quay were closed for the day. It thought I was in a prisoner's yard where our movements were restricted. There was nothing we could do about it.

We departed sharply at 6 PM, thinking that Piraeus would magically appear. However, our hopes were dashed once again when we stopped at Naxos. Our compatriots asked to remain here. The Greek authorities denied them to stay. A repetition of Karpathos. I estimated that Naxos may have had many more refugees crammed in like sardines.

I understood and sympathized with my fellow refugees, who were frightened regarding their future. None of us could imagine what we would confront within the days ahead. Not knowing made it even scarier.

I was frustrated and full of anxiety, worrying more about the future of my children than myself. I cried! I cried! I cried! with tears streaming down my cheeks like a waterfall. These tears cleansed my soul and gave me the strength to continue our journey. I didn't want Ioannis and Maria to end up as orphans. I wanted to provide them with a future in their new homeland. My faith in the Virgin Mary and prayers to Jesus was so important to me as we neared Piraeus. I will continue my refugee experience in Athens in a future diary entry.

Melina's story in Greece.

I arrived in Greece with my two young children Ioannis 5 and Maria 6 on a beautiful sunny day in late April or early May 1923. The American ship stopped at St George's Island off Piraeus so that we would be examined by doctors to see if we had any contagious diseases. I cannot explain it, myself and my two children were disease-free. Some divine hand protected us. Others looked a sickly grey with the grim reaper ready to take them to the next world.

It took a long time for all of us to be processed and examined by the authorities. We finally arrived at Piraeus and had no idea where we would end up. We waited on the dock until they came to take us to our new "home." A truck of the Greek Red Cross came to collect us poor souls to begin our new life.

I heard the accommodation for many of our refugee compatriots were in schools, churches, warehouses, factories, tents, and sheds in Piraeus and Athens. Some refugees lived in the Municipal Theater of Athens, with every box occupied.

The living conditions were atrocious with little or no sanitation, overcrowding, leaky buildings, mud, and a collection of puddles of water. Walls had big holes in them, which allowed the cold wind. Many of these folk wore summer clothing, which didn't keep them warm in the bitter winter of 1922-23. Clothes had become rags sewn together to keep them warm. We arrived in the middle of spring when the weather was warming up and initially avoided the winter blast.

Food was scarce with malnutrition, a severe problem. Some people looked like skeletons with some skin covering their emaciated bodies. Others resembled ghosts ready to meet their creator. A once proud and resourceful people had become beggars with no apparent future. I felt like a beggar as well, but my inner voice kept telling me, "keep going, you're children need you, you will succeed eventually." I kept going.

I thank the charity organizations like the American Red Cross, Near East Relief, and the British Save the Children Fund. They provided food, warm clothing, and blankets that helped us survive our ordeal. Many more of our people would have died without their assistance, and one must not forget the charitable people of America and Britain for their generosity.

Dysentry, smallpox, and cholera swept through like a tornado taking with it the elderly and young children. These poor souls were easily prone to disease. We were lucky as these diseases danced around, disappearing into thin air. Again divine intervention helped us and sustained us.

We were accommodated in a refugee camp at the foot of the Acropolis in Athens. Our "home" would be a tent for the next two years. I never imagined that I would end up in a tragic situation like this considering the comfortable life I once enjoyed in Trebizond. A new reality, a tent for a home. The Greek Government gave us two drachmas a day, a little black bread and sometimes a little soup.

Our food rations were never enough to sustain us properly but were grateful for being alive. At least in Greece, we breathed the air of freedom without having to worry about being killed by the Turks. Oh! The freedom you're such a beautiful word. Now I understood what it meant to be free as a bird.

My children got a cold, and I was scared that it might turn into pneumonia. We were very fortunate to have the American Women's Hospital nearby, providing us with free medical care. Doctors' Mabel Elliott and Esther P.Lovejoy did magnificent work tending to the sick in our camp. I remember both of them looking after my children. They were friendly, kind doctors who worked tirelessly in helping their patients. We also had a small pharmacy that dispensed some medications for free. There weren't a lot of medicines, but it certainly helped in saving many lives.

The winter of 1923-4 was freezing with lots of rain and the occasional sprinkle of snow. At least we had warm clothes, warm blankets, and a little potbelly stove stuffed with wood to keep us warm. Wood was not natural to find. However, I walked around the camp and picked up whatever size of the wood I could find for our potbelly stove. There was a fierce competition as one had to get up at the crack dawn to get their wood before anyone else. Otherwise, you would miss out and end up in a fight with your neighbor. I was lucky on this score and was on good terms with everybody.

There were days when I took the children to see the shops in Athens. I spent some of two drachmas buying the children lemonade or ice cream. We did manage to have some leftover change. Many shopkeepers weren't kind to us. They called us names like Tourkosporoi (Turkish seeds), which was hurtful and insulting. They were racists and discriminated against us Asia Minor Greeks.

I cast my mind back to our tent at the Acropolis and remember the Parthenon, that great symbol of our Athenian ancestors. I thought that I would be welcomed in the land of my ancestors but only to be treated as an outcast from another world. I became nostalgic and fondly remembered the good times I enjoyed with my Turkish friends and neighbors in Trebizond. I wish I could return to my old home but knew that was impossible. Trebizond would always be etched in my heart and soul forever.

Come in the middle of 1925, and we finally moved from our tent to Kokkinia in Piraeus. We were given two rooms in a cheaply constructed apartment block. The walls were paper thin that you could easily hear your next-door neighbors conversation. There was poor insulation with extremes of temperature and very little privacy. While it wasn't an ideal situation, at least we had a roof over our heads.

In our apartment block, most of us came from Asia Minor, with the vast majority coming from Smyrna. I made friends with some women whose husbands' had died in Greece or during the Greek-Turkish war. They were widows like me with young children who found it difficult finding work to support our families. Employment for women was irregular, and the men treated us like second class citizens. Male attitudes towards women staying at home looking after the household and the children were prevalent during those days.

I had to find regular work to support my family as my income was spasmodic. I found an old singer sewing machine in the street which a neighbor repaired. I decided to sew and mend clothes for my neighbors for a small fee. In some cases, I sold some for a higher price in the local market. As I started to save a little money, the idea of starting up my own business became my end goal.

My home in Kokkinia

I made my home in Kokkinia, a refugee district of Piraeus, and knew that I would never return to my ancestral home in Trebizond. Kokkinia became my new place of identity. Our small two-room apartment had paper-thin walls where I could hear my neighbors' conversations. Everyone knew each other's secrets. So much for privacy. The insulation was inferior, suffering the extremes of cold and hot weather.

In the early days, my apartment was sparsely furnished. Our kitchen area was small, with a table and three chairs where we sat down to eat our food. I bought food daily from the local market since we didn't have an ice chest. I stored non-perishable items in a small cupboard. The kitchen was also our place of receiving visitors. Some ladies would visit me to drink coffee and to hear the latest gossip. There was one particular elderly lady named Pagona, originally from Sinope, Asia Minor, who knew everyone's secrets. She would tell me everything to the last detail. I kept these stories to myself and wasn't interested in spreading rumors about my neighbors.

The bedroom had three beds side-by-side where we slept. There was an iconostasis with the Virgin Mary in the corner of the room. I would light the candle every night for protection and to bring us good fortune. Despite our difficulties, I felt that good luck would smile upon us in due course, which it did. My orthodox faith was my guiding light, which I never wavered.

One day as I was walking back from the market, I was in a daze, and from the corner of my right eye, I spotted an old shining black Singer sewing machine which was in a precarious place. Yet the beauty of this bright black machine attracted my attention like a magnet. This machine proved to be a goldmine allowing me to make and repair clothes for our neighbors for a small fee. Leftover garments were sold at the local market for a high price. I must say that people were happy to pay a higher price and were impressed with the quality of the work produced. I learned my sewing skills in Trebizond, where I mended clothes for my Greek and Turkish neighbors and friends.

The money that I saved was spent towards improving the apartment and also looking to starting up a small sewing business. I rearranged the flat to fit two additional small tables with vases of beautiful roses. I was brightening the dull grey background, which added life to our flat. However, I decided to have the apartment painted a bright pink color to give it a more homely appearance. Getting it painted was an ordeal in itself. The landlord ignored my requests as he was only interested in collecting his rent. Well! I kept badgering him until he finally caved in. He murmured about the cost of getting the apartment painted but knew that I was relentless in getting the job completed. My friends commented on how nice the apartment looked after it had been painted.

Finding and renting a small shop was trying for a woman before World War 2. I knew some married women who had their leased premises due to their husbands acting as guarantors. Since I was a widow, the bank would not lend me money thinking I would never repay them. Applying for a bank loan getting would have been easier if Constantine had been alive. Women endured discrimination during the interwar years. Things weren't better even after the war.

I wanted to move to one of the better areas of Athens or Piraeus. I worked long hours to save as much money as I could to buy a house with a lovely garden and beautiful furniture. As much as I dreamed of owning my own home, the bank refused to lend me despite having saved a reasonable deposit. I couldn't do anything about it and continued to live and work out from our rented apartment.

On one occasion, I made an appointment with the bank manager to discuss the possibility of obtaining a loan in my name. I wore my best dress and shoes to make the best possible impression on the bank manager. He was a stern-looking man who thought I was a peasant. Little did he know that I once enjoyed a good lifestyle in Turkey before our expulsion. My loan request was declined.

I made friends with many of the women inside and outside our apartment. Most of them were widows who came from Smyrna, with very few being from Trebizond. Some would visit me, and I would visit them. We were nostalgic about the good old days remembering our parents, husbands, and neighbors who, in some cases, never made it to Greece. We told tales of how we survived our long marches across mountains, deserts and rivers, and the raging fire of Smyrna. I believe it was our fierce determination to survive and the belief in the Virgin that brought us here to Kokkinia.

We never depended on government assistance and established our neighborhood networks. We maintained our Asia Minor identity, developed our own community life, and helped one another. The only thing we had in common with the local Greeks is that we shared a common language and religion. Otherwise, they did not want to know us.

Our neighborhood lacked paved roads, central sewage, and piped water. There were no parks for our children to play. The streets were their playground. At least they were free to play without facing death or being molested by the Turks. Some were too young to remember what happened to their families. Others remembered the trauma they endured with their families until they reached Greece.

Our apartment had no running water, and I would go myself, send the children, or sometimes we would go together to fetch water from a public tap some distance from our home. Many times we queued up until our turn came to fill up our pitchers or jugs. It was unimaginable in the 20th century to obtain water like this. Never had such a problem in Trebizond.

The church was an important place to meet for Sunday mass or celebrate a patron saints day. It is here where I usually met most of my friends. The men often were at the kafenio (coffee house) drinking coffee, discussing politics, or playing cards. I attended the funerals of good friends who passed away and consoled surviving family members. Family and friends comforted me when I lost my husband in 1921.

I remember the following churches: St Evgenios, St Andreas, St Anne, St Michael and St Sophia in Trebizond. Who knows whether these churches were torn down or converted into Mosques. In Kokkinia, I attended St Nicholas, which wasn't too far from home.

As war clouds gathered over Europe, I became pessimistic regarding our future. I didn't want a repetition of 1922. I wanted my children to avoid seeing war and not experience what I did. I couldn't control my future, but things unraveled. I will continue my story.

The final chapter of my life.

I have lived in Greece since 1923 and survived my deportation from Asia Minor, the Second World War, and the Civil War with brother killing brother. The final chapter of my life is straight from my diary. I recorded the events of the 1930s and beyond for my children and grandchildren.

It was an exciting time living in Greece during the 1930s experiencing the Great Depression, the death of Eleftherios Venizelos, the rise of Ioannis Metaxas, the return of the monarchy, and the turbulent 1940s. I will explain these events as I saw them.

Before I delve into my story, I would like to say something about Eleftherios Venizelos. I know he was regarded as a national hero, especially by his fellow Cretans and many from Asia Minor. I respected him as a national leader but did nothing for us, Pontians, when we needed help against the Turks. He told our delegation in Paris to join up with the Armenians instead, and the Greek army never came to protect us. Enough said about Venizelos.

During the great depression, I did quite well compared to other women in my apartment whose husbands became unemployed and who struggled to survive on meager government welfare. There were single women with children who worked seasonally or whenever their employer needed them. I survived by sewing and repairing clothes for neighbors and friends and selling any surplus in the local neighborhood market on weekends. I reduced my prices to make it possible for people to pay me. Sometimes I gave credit to those I trusted and knew they would pay me later. It was sad seeing men going to the kafenio near our apartment in mid-mornings to drink coffee, discuss politics, and the employment situation with friends. Many male customers told me of their frustration, anger, and financial difficulties in trying to support their families. Such stories broke my heart. I considered myself lucky that I was able to earn a good income to support my life in such troubled economic times.

My children Ioannis and Maria were now teenagers. They appreciated everything I did for them. On some weekends, we caught the train from near our apartment and spent our day visiting friends and doing some window shopping in Athens. The children enjoyed their time playing with their friends during our visits. Other times, we spent our day at the beaches of Piraeus or near Athens. The children enjoyed swimming during our hot summers. They were darn, good swimmers. It was beautiful seeing their happy faces.

Both children were doing well in school, almost getting perfect grades. I wanted them to do something useful with their lives. I hoped Ioannis would go to university to study law or medicine. These two professions could earn him a top income allowing him to rise on the Greek socioeconomic ladder. That was still a few years away.

Things were somewhat different for Maria. I wanted her to have a career if she desired one. It wasn't crucial for girls to have an education. However, women seeking a job were frowned upon by Greek men during those dark years. They believed that a woman's place was in the home, cooking, having children, and being loyal wives to their husbands. In 1940, Maria married this nice young man, Kostas Maniades, who was born in Trebizond. I didn't know his family in Trebizond, but at least she married one of our Mikrasiates. She ended up having three sons with Kostas, who survived the 1940s.

On the other hand, Ioannis was about to start university in the autumn of 1940 when war intervened with us fighting the Italians. He fought in the Albanian front with distinction and later transferred to the Middle East. He fought at El Alamein against the Germans and, like Kosta, survived the 1940s. After the Civil War, Ioannis enrolled at

Athens University to study law. On completion, he worked for a major law firm dealing with property issues in Athens.

In 1957, Ioannis took a vacation to the USA and returned home full of new optimism. He met an old school friend Frank Lalatidis in Chicago, who told him that he could make a lot of money in America. Well! Ioannis told Frank that he would begin his immigration formalities upon his return to Greece. His smile beamed from ear to ear. Since Ioannis spoke English with an accent, including having a legal background, his application would quickly get approved. It took about five or six months for him to receive the green light to go to America.

As a mother, I was sad to see him go but also wanted his happiness. On our last night together as a family, I prepared a special dinner and bought the best Greek wine to toast for his future success. We reminisced about the good and bad times we endured as a family. The memory that brought the most discussion was going to the beach. Ioannis thought it was the best time of his life without a shadow of a doubt. The next morning, we went to the airport to see him off. Our last goodbye was a sad affair crying, hugging, and kissing each other. Finally, he boarded his Pan American flight bound for New York. As the big silver bird ascended into the sky, my thoughts took me back to 1922. At least, Ioannis knew his final destination was staying with his friend Lalatidis for a short time.

He migrated to America to begin a new life where he later opened up his law firm in Chicago. Initially, he was required to do some law subjects at the University of Chicago to learn about the US legal system. He passed his bar examination with flying colors. I was proud of his achievement. He got work with one of Chicago's leading Greek-American law firm specializing in property and helped clients with property matters in Greece. His Greek- American compatriots loved him.

I remember August 4, 1936, like it was yesterday. Ioannis Metaxas became dictator of Greece arresting all communists and their sympathizers. Some men in our apartment who supported the Greek Communist Party were arrested and interned in prisons on the Greek mainland and islands. I kept my political views to myself, thus avoiding any potential trouble with the authorities. It was a frightening time in Greece.

The next thing we read in the press is the return of the monarchy. I never liked the Greek monarchy as I believe the Royalists were at fault for us losing Asia Minor and never sending troops to protect us in Pontus. It seemed that Metaxas and King George got on very well with each other. You had nothing to fear as long as you go about your business quietly. Yes! I remained quiet and continued to earn my living unmolested.

In October 1940, we were at war with Italy. Metaxas's response of NO to the Italian ultimatum was a brave decision that made me proud to be Greek. My son, Ioannis, immediately enlisted in the army, and his letters from the different theatres of war described the futility of war. Parts of his letters were censored. I sensed that he was disgusted with all the killing going on around him. He was one of the lucky ones who returned home unaffected by the war.

For me, conflict of the 1940s brought back memories of our war with the Kemalists. I thought that by coming to Greece, I would avoid war. Maria and I had difficult times as both Ioannis and Kostas were fighting the Germans and the Italians. I prayed for both of them to return safely home. Our prayers were answered in the affirmative.

Maria lived with me during the war. We both comforted each other at a time when other women in our apartment received notification of the death of their sons or husbands. As a mother, I understood and felt their grief and always expected to receive bad news. Fortunately, we were lucky. I always thought that a divine hand protected us.

The money that I saved during the 1930s helped us survive the German occupation. We paid inflated prices for scarce food. The Germans patrolled the streets and avoided contact as much as possible with them. They maltreated us and, at times, worse than the Turks. The Germans considered themselves superior to us. Someone told me they were the master race. I wasn't sure what that meant. I always tried to treat everyone the same.

We had no Greek Jews living in our neighborhood but heard that these poor souls were being deported en masse from Salonika and other towns and cities to undisclosed locations in Europe. If the Germans caught us hiding Jews, we risked execution or some severe punishment. I was shocked to learn about the fate of these poor people at the end of the war. I couldn't believe that we could do such horrible things to our fellow human beings.

Of course, the civil war was another tragic period when brothers killed brothers. I am glad the communists got rebuffed, and democracy won in the end. The 1950s were a stressful time, but at least conflict receded into the dustbin of history as we rebuilt our lives once again. On January 1, 1960, I kept my promise never to write in my diary. My journey ends here.

I hope one day, my children will make the final diary after I am gone.

CHAPTER 3

HARRY MULVANEY: OUR MAN IN THE NEAR EAST 1859-1898 PART 1

My name is Harry Mulvaney, an American journalist and diplomat, born in Fairville, New York, in 1859. I attended the University of Chicago and graduated with a degree in ancient Greek and Roman literature. I learned classical Greek and Latin during my studies. I was so fascinated with the classics that I obtained a doctorate from the same university. On completion of my studies, I needed work. It wasn't comfortable finding one, so I found one working as a journalist for the Chicago Times-Herald in 1886.

During my seven years as a reporter, I covered crime, political, and social issues. I had an opportunity to report on the tiny Greek community located on Halstead, Harrison, and Blue Island Streets, where young men and boys toiled long hours to earn enough to pay their rent and remit money to their parents in Greece. Some managed to purchase a pushcart selling fruit, vegetables, and candy to the public. Most of them spoke little or no English and were illiterate in their native tongue.

Initially, there were suspicious of me. It took me a while to win the confidence of the Greeks. I befriended two Greeks named Giorgos and Stathis, who spoke broken English. They acted as intermediaries between their small community and me. They were surprised that I understood and spoke to them in Greek. It made communication so much easier between us. I was able to learn first-hand the racism, discrimination, and xenophobia that these poor Greek immigrants faced in America. It was an eye-opener for me.

In 1892, my newspaper assigned me to cover the presidential election campaign. I wrote a series of articles on the presidential race and received positive feedback from the Democratic Party. My news editor was delighted with the quality of my reports, which contained lots of useful information for our readers. I was very pleased with myself. These articles would trigger my future diplomatic career.

I received a letter out of the blue from the State Department nominating me as US Consul in Athens, Greece. I found out that President Grover Cleveland nominated me for this strategic position. The President invited me to the White House, where he congratulated me on my diplomatic appointment. The President told me that he read my articles with great interest, and my knowledge of Greek would be a great asset for our nation in Greece. I believe I was among a handful of our diplomats at the time who spoke a foreign language.

In June 1893, I caught the steamship, Alexander, to Piraeus from New York, which took ten days. We stopped briefly in Brindisi, Italy, for several hours to stretch our legs. I stopped off at this cafe along the waterfront for coffee, where I got a chance to speak Italian. I hurried back to our ship and off to Greece. I disembarked in Piraeus and immediately proceeded to the US Legation to meet our Minister, John

Myers. He briefed me on my duties and the current political situation in Greece. The next day, I went to the palace at Tatoi to present my diplomatic credentials to King George 1. He warmly received me and was pleasantly surprised that I answered him in Greek. We became good friends and was a regular visitor to the palace.

My visits to the palace were private and had nothing to do with my diplomatic status. The King and I discussed the uneasy political situation that existed in the Balkans and on Crete. The last-named place would explode into a short-lived conflict between Greece and the Ottoman Empire in 1897.

His Majesty was very interested in American democracy and wanted our two nations to forge close diplomatic relations. I was in favor of this but couldn't go against the instructions of the State Department, who wished to no involvement in European affairs. Our nation loved its splendid isolation until our war with Spain in 1898. Our battle with Spain came as a surprise to me but felt sympathetic for the Cubans seeking their independence. In some way, the Cuban struggle for independence reminded me of the Greeks who fought valiantly against the Ottoman empire some 75 years earlier.

Besides my consular duties, I visited some of the ancient sites outside Athens, which brought home famous old Greek names like Homer, Sophocles, Aristophanes, Plato, Socrates, and Aristotle to mind. I visited the Epidaurus theater in Peloponnesus and imagined attending one of Aristophanes's famous plays. The acoustics were simply divine. I also visited the Parthenon, which overlooked Athens. I imagined listening to Pericles delivering his funeral oration for the war dead. For me, the Parthenon symbolized the birthplace of democracy, which our founding fathers modeled our American nation. We owe so much to the ancient Greeks.

Around this time, there was the talk of staging the first modern Olympic Games in Athens. Imagine seeing this event during my time as US Consul in Athens. The excitement was building up as we approached the official opening to the first modern Olympiad. On April 6, 1896, the Panathinaikos Stadium overflowed with spectators, with King George 1 declaring the official opening to the first modern Summer Olympic Games. Our American athletes won medals in track and field, which made me very happy.

For the Greeks, Spiron Louis winning the marathon brought honor to the small Hellenic Kingdom. I remember when Louis was presented with his silver medal and olive branch by the King. He was so proud and smiling from ear-to-ear. At last, the Greeks heard their national anthem being played and sang along with it. It was a fantastic moment and got goosebumps hearing the Greeks singing their national song. Momentarily, I thought I was Greek too.

After a successful Olympic Games, war clouds were appearing on the horizon. There were rumblings in Crete where the Greeks there wanted union with the motherland. The island belonged to the Ottoman Empire, who were reluctant to relinquish it to the Greeks. However, Greek nationalists in Crete and Athens wanted the union to proceed as quickly as possible. In the end, this resulted in a short war between the Greeks and Turks, which lasted six weeks. The intervention of the major European powers established peace between the belligerents, and the Greeks paid war reparations to the Turks. It proved a humiliating defeat for the Greeks, and King George was lucky to escape an assassination attempt on his life.

Some Greeks came from America to fight the Turks. The war had finished by the time they arrived and missed out on defending their homeland. Some decided to remain in Greece, while others wanted to return to America. I issued the visas for their return. A handful of

American citizens of Greek background who came to fight didn't go down too well with Americans back home. Americans thought that you couldn't have loyalties to two nations. I sympathized with our American citizens of Greek origin who came to defend the land of their birth. However, I couldn't publicly display my personal feelings since the US had no direct involvement in this conflict.

In June 1898, the State Department recalled me back to the US and so ended my first diplomatic posting. I thoroughly enjoyed my time in Athens, and I am grateful that I undertook classics at the University of Chicago. I fell in love with Greece and its people, which made me an ardent philhellene, something that would remain for the rest of my life. My diplomatic journey will continue in my next piece.

Harry Mulvaney:
Return to America and back to the
Near East 1898-1906 Part 2

I returned to America in late June 1898 and took a few weeks off to recuperate from my sea journey to New York. I took the opportunity to catch up with family and friends in Fairville. I received a letter from the Chicago Times-Herald offering me the position of literary editor. An area I always desired when I worked for that newspaper. The newspaper told me to start after summer giving me a chance to do some sightseeing in our beautiful New England states.

In September, I started my new position as a literary editor and am pleased the management gave me a free hand to write pieces on the classics. This gave me the chance to promote the ancient Greek and Roman classics to our readers. Many readers wrote to me personally thanking me for my articles and book reviews. I suppose the newspaper was encouraged to have a former Consul on its editorial staff. The next three years were a delight, which also allowed me to write two books on my experiences in Greece.

The books sold well and received very favorable reviews in the New York Times and other US newspapers. These books helped me, which I shall explain later. In 1901, the Chicago Times-Herald became known as the Chicago American, where I continued in the same position until my resignation in December 1903. Even with the name change, the new owners never interfered with my column.

I resigned from my position, not from a lack of job dissatisfaction, but wanted a new direction in my life. I seized the opportunity to go on speaking tours earning a good income talking about my books. Audiences were very appreciative of my presentations given at well-known universities and church halls across America. There was great interest shown by people wishing to learn about ancient Greece and Rome from the recent archaeological discoveries. I became known as some major speaking celebrity.

My life took a new direction promoted as US Consul-General in Athens in early 1905 and was thrilled to be back in the land of Pericles. I continued my private visits to the palace discussing the major political events of the day with King George. We sipped our brandy and smoked our Havana cigars until late into the evening before heading back to our Legation.

The political situation in Greece and the Balkans was fluid. A few examples in Greek politics to be cited for illustrative purposes. The Prime Minister, Theodore Deliyannis, was murdered by a professional gambler at the main entrance of the Chamber of Deputies as revenge for the passing of strict laws against gambling houses. Deliyannis was a political firebrand who could move his audiences, even his opponents, to the home of the Olympian Gods. The country mourned the loss of its popular premier. Athenians wanted to lynch the culprit.

Crete was another issue that caused problems for Greece. The Cretans were always pushing for union with the motherland, which brought Greece into conflict with Turkey and the great European powers (Britain, France, Russia, Germany, Italy, and Austro-Hungary). Prince George of Greece, appointed as the High Commissioner for Crete by the major powers, was keen to promote the idea of union with Greece. However, his efforts fell on deaf ears. The European powers wished to preserve the delicate balance of power on the continent and to maintain the Ottoman Empire as long as possible. They didn't want a European war over Crete.

In 1905-06, the political situation in Macedonia was highly explosive, which could have erupted anytime into a Balkan War. The British Minister in Athens, Sir Edward Leonard, explained to me that the European powers wanted this region pacified thus dampening down any prospects of conflict. Greece, Serbia, and Bulgaria coveted Macedonia by setting up schools with each promoting their language and culture to the mixed populations that inhabited this region.

The operation of Greek, Bulgarians, and Serbian bands in Macedonia resulted in civilian casualties, including the burning of villages, which proved a major headache for the European powers. The hatred between Greeks and Bulgarians and Serbians and Bulgarians was intense. Muslims committed atrocities against Christians in Macedonia too. The Ottoman army did everything in its power to stop these bands from crossing onto its territory. I heard that the Greek, Bulgarian, and Serbian governments were secretly aiding and encouraging these bands to create chaos and panic in Macedonia. Athens, Belgrade, and Sofia were warned by the powers to stop giving material aid to these bands. The Balkan states ignored these warnings.

We had good relations with the Greek government. There was one issue that needed rectification before it became a significant issue between our two countries. Our Minister in Athens, Peter Hammond, and I were invited by the Greek Foreign Minister, Alexandros Skouzes, to discuss Greek migration to America. Some Greeks headed for St Louis were denied entry by US Immigration in New York. Skouzes wanted to know why these individuals were denied entry, whereas others went to Boston, Chicago, or Los Angeles without any problem. We showed him copies of correspondence exchanged between the Secretary of Commerce and Labor and the State Department that these individuals entry violated the foreign contract labor laws. He wasn't happy with this decision but accepted the right of our country to deny entry to such individuals. Skouzes told us that he would ensure that Greeks migrating were to be informed of the strict US immigration and labor laws to avoid such future occurrences.

I learned that there was a Greek named Nicholas Tsouvalis of Boston who acted as a labor agent for various US companies. They wanted cheap unskilled labor to work in their steel and railroad companies, and coal mines. His role was to attract young Greek males to work in these places with or not official documents. Some of them complained to one Greek-American newspaper that they were being underpaid for their work. The paper found out that Tsouvalis was charging a fee deducted out of the workers' wages for providing a so-called service. This matter was brought to the attention of the US Immigration Bureau, who prosecuted and deported Tsouvalis back to Greece.

The happiest event for us was the Athens Olympic Games staged between April 22-May 2, 1906. It brought back beautiful memories of 1896 all over again. Our athletes arrived several days before the official opening of the games with our Olympic committee headed by Jimmy B.Smith. King George officially opened the games before 70,000 spectators. The Greek and American athletes received thunderous applause from the crowd when they entered the stadium. Our athletes won the respect of the Greeks by not arguing with the judges, accepting the competition rules, and displaying good sportsmanship towards their fellow athletes. The New York Times reported that "the King gave a gala dinner of 400 in honor of foreign delegates, athletes committee, judges and winners" at the palace. President Theodore Roosevelt sent a congratulatory telegram to Smith and athletes for their performance at the games.

Later that year, I was recalled back to the US and would spend the next two years writing books and giving public speeches.

Harry Mulvaney Part 3: 1906-1909

Upon my return to the US in June 1906, I took the opportunity to visit family and friends in Fairville. We had some enjoyable family outings to a beautiful park with a nearby lake. Some family members and friends asked me what it was like to be a diplomat. I couldn't divulge state secrets to them. I spoke to them in general terms that being an American diplomat was an honor and a privilege to represent our nation abroad. I had the honor of meeting diplomats of other nations and attending parties hosted by the host country or the Embassy in the capital where we were accredited.

Until my next diplomatic posting, I went back on the lecture tour and writing a couple of new books. My public lectures focused on the 1906 Olympic Games, visiting ancient Greek sites and stories about my diplomatic work, which the audiences enjoyed listening too. I received favorable book reviews in the New York Times, Boston Globe, and Washington Post for my latest publications, which helped boost their sales.

In early June 1908, I was appointed US Consul General in Constantinople, which would keep me busy for the next two years. The journey to the Ottoman capital took ten days from New York traveling onboard the Olympia stopping off in Marseilles and Piraeus along the way. I spent a couple of days in Athens doing some sightseeing and catching up with old friends. Our warship, the USS Abraham Lincoln, took us to Constantinople to begin my new diplomatic post.

As our ship entered the Bosphorus in a northerly direction, I could see Scutari, the Asiatic Port, on my right and Constantinople to my left. After a short distance, we entered the Golden Horn, where our ship anchored at Galata. I could see the bridge connecting Galata with Constantinople. There were ships of many nations entering and exiting the Golden Horn with some destined for ports on the Black Sea. I never traveled to the Black Sea cities of Sinope, Samsoun, and Trebizond, which contained large Greek communities. Some of our missionaries who worked in these places told me that they were able to carry out their work unmolested.

I disembarked and was taken to our Embassy to meet our Ambassador, Charles Bicknell, who explained the internal situation in the Ottoman Empire and its relations with its neighbors. In July, the empire was shaken to its core of what called was the Young Turk revolution, a movement composed of army officers who demanded the restoration of the 1876 Constitution, which Sultan Abdul Hamid 11had initially suspended some 32 years earlier. Their slogan was "Long live the fatherland, long live the nation, long live liberty," which captured the imagination of all the subjects of the empire. Both Muslims and Christian embraced and hugged each other, thinking that a new era was about to begin.

Facing a revolt, the Sultan acceded to the demands of his officers in restoring the 1876 constitution and the staging of elections. Elections took place in November and December 1908 with the Committee of Union and Progress winning the bulk of the seats in the Ottoman Chamber. The Greeks, Armenians, and Jews were each granted representation in the Chamber based on the size of their population. At last, they had a voice in the affairs of the empire, which wasn't too last very long.

In April 1909, Abdul Hamid's counter-coup failed. As army officers revolted once again, forcing him to resign his throne to Mehmed V., I spoke with local Greeks and Armenians who were happy with Abdul Hamid no longer in charge of imperial affairs, and parliament could function normally. The minorities had been transformed from subjects into citizens with equal rights with Muslims.

Many Muslims pondered over the idea of Christians attaining equality with them. Abdul Hamid exploited these Muslim fears, which contributed in some respects to the Armenian massacres in Adana. However, the interplay of political, economic, and religious differences also contributed to this tragedy. The Armenians were considered the wealthiest and most successful element in Adana. In Hadjin and Mersina, the Armenians were massacred along with their houses burned by Turkish mobs. The Young Turks investigated the Armenians massacres with court-marshals handing down death sentences to over 100 Turks and 7 Armenians. At this stage, the action of the Young Turks was well received the Greeks and Armenians. On the other hand, Turkish reactions to the sentences were mixed.

We received reports from our missionaries and consuls in the Adana region, stating that our schools, hospitals, and orphanages were untouched during the massacres. We were pleased to hear that the Ottoman authorities did everything in their power to protect our institutions from the mobs. The British and French Consuls also furnished us with reports of what happened in Adana. These reports were forwarded to the State Department.

Besides the political developments, I enjoyed the social life in Constantinople. I visited the Aghia Sophia on numerous occasions and admired its architectural beauty and imagined being transported back in time to the Byzantium Emperors, who attended mass here. It would have been something special seeing the Patriarch delivering his sermon to his flock. My visits to the Dolmabache and Topkaki Palaces, the Sultan Ahmed, Mosque, and the bazaars were memorable.

The bazaars were busy places with people seeking to buy merchandise from sellers at bargain prices. You would witness sellers and buyers haggling over price, which is the custom in this part of the world. One day, I passed by a stall when the owner said to me, "please come, sir, I give you a special price for this handmade rug." I pretended to show interest but told him, "no, thanks." "Please, effendi, I give you an even lower price," he said. He gave up in the end.

I made friends with my British and French counterparts, including some influential members of the Young Turk government. Sometimes we socialized over dinner in the most excellent restaurants owned by Greeks discussing the political issues of the day and telling jokes. The Turks loved telling us funny quips, which made us cry from laughter. Our conversation was mostly conducted in French, which forced me to learn it. Over time, I became proficient both in French and Turkish.

The diplomatic garden parties were one of the main events on the social calendar. It allowed interacting with fellow diplomats and members of the Ottoman Government. Some of the Embassies overlooked the Golden Horn, which provided a spectacular view of the city.

In November 1909, I was notified by the State Department that I would be transferred to Salonika to commence my duties in March 1910. I returned for a short vacation to America.

Harry Mulvaney 1910-13: Part 4

I returned to America just before Christmas of 1909 spend it with my family in Fairville, New York. Surprisingly, the weather was mild for winter with no snow. It felt strange not seeing snow at Christmas time like former times. Never mind, I enjoyed my stay and looked forward to 1910 with anticipation. I wondered what surprises Salonika would hold for me.

I left America in early March 1910 to be America's Consul General in Salonika, which was still under Ottoman rule. I commenced my duties on March 30, which were to prove very interesting over the next two years or so. I had very little time for socializing, as political events kept me very busy. Salonika was a cosmopolitan city inhabited by Jews, Turks, Greeks, Bulgarians, Armenians, and others. The Jews were the most significant element in the city, with trade almost entirely in the hands of Jewish traders.

Salonika was the key to the Balkans with three railway lines serving Belgrade, Monastir, and Constantinople directly. It was the second city of the Empire in the Balkans behind the capital, Constantinople. This city was a hotbed of revolutionary activity with the Internal Macedonian Revolutionary Organization (IMRO) established in 1897, the Greek Macedonian Committee in 1903, and the Young Turk movement, which forced Sultan Abdul Hamid to restore the 1876 constitution in 1908. I also was informed that the Greek and Bulgarian Consulates were aiding the Greek and Bulgarian bands operating in Macedonia.

Some significant events such as the Albanian revolt, the general situation in Macedonia, the Italo-Turkish war 1911-12, and the commencement of the Balkan Wars occupied a big chunk of my time. All these issues were somehow interlinked with the Young Turks contributing towards the demise of their Empire and sowing the seeds of a future Balkan war. Initially, the Young Turks promised democracy and equality for all its citizens but turned out to be no different from Abdul Hamid.

In Albania, the Young Turks used heavy-handed methods against the Albanians who had proved to be loyal subjects of the Empire and contributed soldiers to the Ottoman army. The Albanians wanted autonomy and to use their language in their daily affairs. An Albanian revolt did occur, which the Turks brutally suppressed. This much angered the Albanians. I received a copy of a manifesto from an Albanian committee that demanded the following from the Ottoman government. It read: 1. All governments officers to be of Albanian birth; 2. the employment of the Albanian language and alphabet in all schools established by the government; 3.amnesty for Albanians sentenced for political offenses; 4. the introduction of foreign capital; 5. reopening off all Albanian schools closed down by the government; 6. removing the embargo of all newspapers and other publications.

The Albanian grievances were legitimate, but the Turks weren't interested in taking action to improve the situation. They wrongly thought that as fellow Muslims, they would be satisfied with their lot. The British and French Consuls informed me that the Albanians were hoping the European powers would intervene on their behalf, which never eventuated. As an American, I was concerned that our missionary schools in Albania would operate freely and not closed down by the Turks.

A group of our missionaries visited me in Salonica to ascertain what would happen if our schools were closed down in Albania. I told them that I would contact our Minister in Constantinople for further instructions on this matter. Several days later, the missionaries returned to ask me how the issue was progressing. I told them that

I would speak with Ottoman authorities to ensure that our schools remained open. One missionary suggested that US marines be posted as guards to protect our schools. As much as I favored this idea, we had to respect the laws of the Ottoman empire.

In Macedonia, the situation was like a cauldron ready to explode at any time. The Ottoman government pressed its neighbors to stop the Greek and Bulgarian bands from conducting raids onto its territory. There were rumors that the Young Turks encouraged the formation of Turkish bands to torture and terrorize Christians in Chalkidiki and other parts of Macedonia. This formation was to counteract the actions of the Bulgarian and Greek bands. I received reports from our Consul in Monastir that the Turks had used force against the Christians in that city. Troops occupied all streets. Turkish authorities claimed they discovered three documents written by a secret Bulgarian group urging the Christians to surrender useless arms to police, and anyone who violated this order would be punished and executed in secret. The second document stated that a state of siege would be proclaimed in the Vilayet of Monastir, and finally, the assassination of prominent Young Turks would be carried out.

Whether these documents were authentic or not, Turkish troops molested Greek and Bulgarian peasants, which I know angered the Greek and Bulgarian governments. Both governments were ill-prepared for war and also had their differences over the future settlement of Macedonia.

While Macedonia kept bubbling away, the Italo-Turkish war raised the passions of Turks in Salonika. Many young Turks rushed to enlist in the army, who were ready to go to Tripoli. I met the Italian Consul, Count Amaro, to ascertain his views of the conflict. He told me that Italy had ambitions to be a colonial power alongside Britain and France in the Mediterranean. Italian commercial activity in Tripoli angered the Arabs, whereas the Turks disliked the Italians getting a foothold there. Moreover, Amaro stated Italy wished to remove the stigma of its defeat at Adowa to the Ethiopians in 1896. They were shocked, losing to an African nation.

I read press reports of the Italian navy shelling Beirut and the outer forts at the entrance of the Dardanelles in February and April 1912, respectively. Italy occupied the Dodecanese in May 1912, which concerned the British. They didn't want another European power occupying these islands, which were close to their strategic interests in the eastern Mediterranean and the Suez Canal. My British colleague conveyed the importance of getting the Italians to leave the Dodecanese. Whether the Italians would go or not was best left for the Europeans and the Turks to resolve.

As the Balkan states were ready to declare war on the Ottoman Empire in early October 1912, the Treaty of Lausanne was signed at Ouchy, establishing peace between the Turks and Italians.

Harry Mulvaney Part 5: the Balkan Wars 1912-13

As quickly as the ink dried with the signing of the Treaty of Lausanne (1912), establishing peace between the Ottoman Empire and Italy, the Balkan League (Greece, Montenegro, Serbia, and Bulgaria) marched off to war against the Ottoman Empire in October 1912. Our ambassador in Constantinople informed me on the eve of the Balkan conflict that Washington extended my stay as Consul General in Salonika for another 12 months. I was surprised at the extension. Anyway, I was beginning to enjoy my role as the senior US diplomat in the second most important European city of the Ottoman Empire.

With the declaration of war, events moved so fast that I had very little time to absorb them as the Balkan League scored spectacular military successes against the Turks. The entire diplomatic corps in Salonika couldn't believe that the Turks collapsed so quickly with the Bulgarian army pushing close to the gates of Constantinople. The Greeks had their moment of celebration in occupying Salonika before the Bulgarians who were very upset over this prize of war. Salonika would prove a bone of contention between these two allied partners. The Bulgarians believed it belonged to them.

On November 8, 1912, a triumphant Greek army lead by Crown Prince, Constantine entered Salonika, who was received enthusiastically by the Greek inhabitants who shouted: "Long Live Greece," thus ending nearly 500 years of Ottoman rule. I later learned that we had many US citizens of Greek origin who played an essential role in the Greek victories. These men were not only loyal to the US but hadn't forgotten their Greek roots. However, there were dissenting voices back home, who considered these citizens as having divided loyalties. Privately, I thought these men heroes not traitors but patriots for their former homeland.

Salonika was inhabited by Jews, Turks, Greeks, Bulgarians, and other races. The Jews were by far the most significant element that dominated the local economy of the city. There were Jewish converts to Islam who were known as donmes. Some of them were founding members of the Committee of Union and Progress (Young Turks).

The Greeks entered Salonika one day before the feast day of St Demetrios, whom they regard as the patron saint and protector of the city. I heard the Greeks had prayed to him to liberate them from the Ottoman yoke and believed his heavenly intercessions helped the Greek army achieve its military victories in Yenidje and Pigadia.

I saw from the second floor of our consulate, on November 11, King George entering Salonika to jubilant citizens waving Greek flags, showering the Royal family with flowers and singing the Greek national anthem. It was a moment that I shall never forget. The next day, Constantinos Ractivan, the Minister of Justice, arrived in Salonika. I took the opportunity to arrange a meeting with him to discuss how the Greek occupation would impact our educational and commercial interests in Salonika and Macedonia generally. He assured me that our national interests would be protected in areas under Greek control. He couldn't guarantee the actions of his Serbian and Bulgarian partners towards American interests in their respective military zones. However, I received assurances from the Serb and Bulgarian military commanders that they would protect our institutions within their designated zones.

The first Balkan war continued as the Bulgarians pinned the Turks onto the Chatalja line and looked poised to enter the Constantinople. However, the spread of cholera and dysentery amongst the combatants resulted in many deaths on both sides. On the other hand, the Russians weren't keen seeing the Bulgarians occupying Constantinople, which they always wanted to possess.

I received reports from the British Consul and our Consuls in Macedonia of atrocities - rape, robbery, and massacres committed mainly by irregulars and, in some cases, troops from all combatants against innocent Christian and Muslim populations. I understood troops fighting against each other, but the targeting of civilians was inexcusable. All stories of massacres and other crimes were to be investigated by an international commission headed by leading jurists.

The Greek navy played an essential role in the conflict by blockading the coast of Epirus from the Gulf of Arta to Avlona Bay. Furthermore, the islands of Thasos, Samothrace, Imbros, Lemnos, Tenedos, and Psara came under Greek control. These islands were mainly Greek populated with its inhabitants demanding union with Greece. The Peace Treaty of London of May 1913 negotiated between the great European powers, and the Balkan League left some unresolved issues such as the disposition of the Aegean islands and Bulgaria's dissatisfaction regarding Macedonia.

Our Minister in Athens informed me that conversations among foreign representatives of the great powers there favored Salonika becoming a free city under international control. I told him that Greece had legitimate claims to the occupied islands, but Salonika was a different matter. Salonika was something that the Balkan states had to work out among themselves. I knew the Greeks would not give up Salonika under no circumstance. They regarded it as rightfully theirs and would be prepared to fight for it. A combined Greek-Serbian force defeated the Bulgarians in June 1913, with Salonika officially incorporated into the Hellenic Kingdom.

The assassination of King George 1 of Greece in March 1913 shook Greece to its core. Greeks couldn't understand why Alexander

Schinas carried out this act against their beloved sovereign. Rumors were circulating in Salonika that the assassin may have in the pay of a foreign power, or the Bulgarians could have been behind it. The Bulgarian premier, Ivan Gueshoff, sent a telegram to Venizelos expressing his condolence in which the former referred to the king as "one of the first authority of our holy alliance." No report was ever issued stating whether Schinas acted alone or involved others. I believe that Schinas acted alone in carrying out the assassination.

Before taking up my next diplomatic posting, the Treaty of Bucharest signed by all the belligerents on August 10, 1913, established peace in the Balkans. Furthermore, the Ottoman government signed two treaties with Bulgaria and Greece in September and November 1913. The former, known as the Treaty of Constantinople, established the frontier between the Ottoman Empire and Bulgaria. In contrast, the latter one saw the Ottoman Empire ceding Macedonia, including Salonica, a large chunk of Epirus, Crete, and the Aegean islands to Greece.

Harry Mulvaney: social and cultural life in Salonika Part 6

I reported in my previous paper the political events, issuing and renewing passports, expanding our commercial interests, ensuring the Ottoman State protected our educational institutions, and later by the Greeks, which were a part of my consular duties. During times when things were quiet, I took the opportunity to ingratiate myself in the social and cultural life of Salonika.

The city was divided up into neighborhoods (mahalas) showing the different races where they lived. The Turks resided in the upper parts of the city, and the Jews inhabited the lower districts near the old sea wall demolished in 1889 and the harbor. The Christians lived along Egnatia Road, and small pockets existed around the cathedral attached to the Vlatadon monastery. Furthermore, the commercial and European quarters were located in the western region of Salonika. It is here where foreign banks: the Bank of Salonika and Imperial Ottoman Bank with their headquarters in Constantinople, whereas the Greek-owned ones: the Bank of Mitylene, Bank of Athens, and the Bank of East were located.

Egnatia Road is a historical thoroughfare where victorious Roman armies, Byzantium Emperors and the Greek army marched into Salonika. In the morning, you see Greeks, Turks, Jews, Bulgarians, Albanians, Hodjas, monks, Catholic priests, and children going about their business on this busy road. In 1911, the Greek community built a fountain in honor of Sultan Mehmed Resat 5th visit to Salonika. I understand his Majesty was very pleased with his subjects' gesture towards him.

Salonika has many schools providing an excellent education for students. The most notable ones are Alliance Israelite Universelle

(Jewish), American Agricultural School, and French Institute of Salonika established in 1904 and 1906, respectively. Our American school was founded by missionaries to teach people farming and trades. The President of our school invited me to attend the graduation ceremonies giving me great delight representing our nation. I gave a short speech before presenting the graduates with their diplomas.

Since the 1890s, the Salonika urban landscape has undergone a massive change. I was a regular visitor to the Allatini, Hatzilazaros, and Capatzi families who lived in the Pyrgos district. The Jewish industrialist Charles Allatini, the owner of a flour mill and brickworks, was the wealthiest person in Salonika. Sultan Abdul Hamid 11 was kept prisoner in Allatini's villa until his escape to Constantinople in 1912. Periklis Hatzilazaros villa provided hospitality to the Greek royal family after the city fell to the Greeks.

They invited me to their social gatherings, where I mixed with the well-to-do citizens of Salonika, where they served sumptuous meals along with the best wines and French champagne. I used these gatherings to gather commercial information that I passed on to our Minister in Constantinople. Such details could help expand our business interests in the Balkans. I can say with great pride that Americans were famous amongst the people of Salonika.

The Jews were concerned over the anti-semitic attacks that took place after the Greek occupation. They feared to be Hellenized, which would result in losing their language and cultural identity. The Greek government responded by introducing reforms that sought to rectify the situation. Some included: preservation of the Sabbath in the city, allowed to keep accounts in their language (Spanish- Jewish/ Landino), and freedom of the press. Many Salonika Jews remained skeptical over Greek intentions.

They worried that they would lose their economic dominance. Some Jews argued that Salonika should either become an international or a free city, which was favored by Austro-Hungary. The latter didn't want Greek possession though a Bulgarian one would have been preferable. Other powers had imperial designs on Salonika. Many Jews jumped ship by becoming citizens of the other countries, and our consulate was busy, too, making extra consular fees. In the end, Salonika became a Greek city much to the disappointment of some sections of the Jewish community.

The Jews were very active in the labor movement. In 1908, Abraham Benaroya founded the Labor Association of Salonika, imbued with socialist ideas. In 1909, the Labor Association, in collaboration with the Socialist Center, established the Labor Socialist Federation of Salonika. On May 1, 1912, the first time workers celebrated Mayday in the Ottoman Empire with most being Jews. The labor movement had their newspapers published in Landino, French, and Italian, which included: Workers Newspaper, Labor Solidarity (the organ of the Federation), Independent, Messagero, and Avanti.

I loved walking along the Salonika quay with its cafes, cabarets, beer- gardens, and music halls. One could hear gypsy violins, Turkish instruments, Greek melodies, and dirty French songs. Sometimes, I would meet the British Consul, Sir Harry Davenport at Barbagiannis restaurant discussing political issues, smoking our Turkish cigarettes, and spinning yarns to pass our time. Davenport was a highly respected by the Turks and foreign diplomatic corps in treating everyone with honesty and fairness. I enjoyed listening to Greek bouzouki music with its songs filled with sadness and happiness, depending on the political mood of the time. Oh! the Turkish belly dancers were something else provocatively shaking their hips.

Along the quay and surrounding streets, hawkers and street sellers were vying for your business. They would come out and try to sell you something for a high price. I would tell them "too expensive' and bargain with them over the amount in their language. It was fun conducting business with such people earning an "honest" living. I qualify "honest," being careful not to be ripped off by these guys.

I could also see the White Tower (previously known as the Tower of Blood) located on Begiaz Avenue, renamed King Constantine Avenue, after the Greek liberation of the city in November 1912. It is one of the best landmarks overlooking the Gulf Salonika. Once upon a time, the guilty were executed inside the tower, where blood flowed freely. The Turks used it as a barracks, and its towers had cannons facing the sea. The tower allowed them to observe and protect the city from an enemy naval attack. It is here Tahsin Pasha, the Turkish Commander, surrendered Salonika to the Greeks. Since the Greek occupation, the White Tower has become an essential symbol for the Greeks.

I visited mosques (Alaca Imaret and Hamza Bey), synagogues (Monastiriotou and Etz Haim), and churches (Saints Demetrios, Gregory Palamas, and Sophia) and admired the beauty of their architecture. The Greeks regard St Demetrios as their original church in Salonika. St Demetrios is viewed as the patron saint of the city. There was a lot of construction of churches in the early years of the Byzantine Empire, and the Turks built their mosques after Salonika fell to them in 1430. The arch of Galerius, the Palace of Galerius, and Hippodrome located on Egnatia Street are significant monuments constructed during the Roman Times.

In my limited time, I learned to appreciate the people, the history and culture of this multiethnic city. You can see the strong Jewish presence in every aspect of its daily life where the Jews have come to accept the Greek control. I am off to my next diplomatic post in Smyrna.

Harry Mulvaney Part 7 1914-18: the War Years

The last three years in Salonika were exciting from a political, cultural, social, and diplomatic standpoint. I saw the Ottoman Empire lose territory, whereas some of the Balkan States, especially, Greece doubled its area and population. I made friends with some of the prominent families of Salonika.

I left Salonika on November 30, 1913, and took a short break visiting Vienna, Berlin, Paris, and London. These were ancient cities steeped in history with their famous landmarks, e.g., State Opera House, Schonbrunn, and Hofburg palaces in Vienna, Brandenburg Gate, and Reichstag building in Berlin, Eiffel Tower and Notre Dame Cathedral in Paris and Buckingham Palace and Houses of Parliament in London. There were so many other landmarks to see but time didn't permit it. In London, I had lunch with our Ambassador and caught up with an old friend, Sir Harry Davenport. Harry and I reminisced about our days as serving diplomats in Salonika. On my return, I stopped off in Rome visited St Peters Basilica, the Coliseum, and other ancient sites appreciating this city's contribution to western civilization. My next stop was a brief stopover in Piraeus before heading off to Smyrna to commence my appointment as US Consul-General on January 1, 1914.

I immediately took a liking to this cosmopolitan city with its precious cultural and social life. It had department stores selling the latest Parisienne women's fashions, fine restaurants where wealthy Greeks, Armenians, and Levantines intermingled with Turkish Pashas, and with its social clubs. Only the rich could afford the annual fees to these social clubs where people in business gathered to socialize and discuss their latest business dealings. Smyrna had many beautiful Christian churches of various denominations, mosques, and synagogues. The market places (bazaars) were a hive of activity with vendors selling fruit, vegetables, clothing, carpets, and rugs. You could hear a babble of foreign languages, which made me feel comfortable as I could speak Greek, Turkish, and French.

When I arrived, the atmosphere was agitated in Smyrna, but the different ethnic groups seemed to have gotten well with each other. Outside Smyrna, in Phocaea, tensions between Greeks and Turks were very high. The situation was made worse with the influx of Muslim refugees from the Balkan Wars who sought accommodation. Local Turks attacked nearby villages, killing, pillaging, and robbing the Greek inhabitants who some fled to the islands off the Anatolian coast, and others sought refuge in Phocaea. Even in Phocaea, the Greeks suffered at the hands of the Turkish mobs.

Rumors of war between Greece and the Ottoman Empire appeared in the daily Smyrna multilingual press. The Greek Premier, Eleftherios Venizelos, proposed a voluntary exchange of populations with Ottoman Grand Vizier in June 1914 who thought it was an excellent solution. The scheme was to go into effect, but the intervention of hostilities in Europe put an end to that. Turkey remained neutral until the end of October.

Once Turkey officially entered the war on the side of Germany and Austro- Hungary, the British, Russian, and French Consuls immediately asked for their passports. I became the Dean of the diplomatic corps in Smyrna, representing British, Russian, and French interests and also assisting their nationals to leave Smyrna. I had a hefty workload trying to do my consular duties plus those of other nations whose interests I represented. I intervened on several occasions on behalf of British or French citizens who were mistreated by the Turkish authorities. The Ottoman Governor, Rahmi Bey, was an amiable person who did everything to protect non-Muslim citizens and foreign nationals in Smyrna. He didn't get on too well with his masters in Constantinople. I struck up a good relationship with him, who protected our American interests.

During 1915, I received reports from our Ambassador in Constantinople with the struggle taking place between the Turks and British Empire at Gallipoli. The death toll was staggering with fierce hand-to-hand fighting to occupy a particular strategic point or hill. I learned that the German General Liman Von Sanders, who commanded the Ottoman army, didn't get on with the Turkish commander, Mustapha Kemal Pasha. Despite their differences, they cooperated to defeat their enemy, which they accomplished in the end.

The Anglo-French navy blockaded the entrance to the Gulf of Smyrna, preventing the Ottoman naval fleet from going to the Dardanelles. Occasionally, the Anglo-French shelled Smyrna, but the Turkish guns returned fire from the outer forts to the entrance of Smyrna harbor. Other parts of the Ottoman Empire suffered severe food shortages, but Smyrna, with its rich hinterland, was spared hunger during the entire war.

I had a heated encounter with Liman Von Sanders in the presence of Rahmi Bey at Government House. He tried to justify the deportation of Greeks and Armenians on the grounds they were traitors to the Ottoman State. I found him to be an arrogant, repulsive, and unsympathetic individual who cared very little for ordinary people. I argued that the Greeks and Armenians were critical to the economy of Smyrna and should be allowed to return to their homes. Rahmi Bey agreed with me. Von Sanders was angry with his deportation order rescinded by Rahmi Bey. The German responded proudly, "how dare a Turk to cancel an order of a German officer" and stormed out, shaking his head. I kept my cool throughout our exchange. "Good riddance," I said and never saw him again.

In April 1917, the US declared war against Germany but severed its relations with the Ottoman Empire. We needed to protect our institutions and missionaries operating in Turkey during the war. I hoped Germany would receive a military whipping from us and never forgot my exchange with Von Sanders. I believed that all German officers were like him, but my views changed at the end of hostilities. I met some German POW officers in Salonika who told me that they were disgusted with some of their colleagues who did nothing to stop the massacres of Christians in Turkey. They said to me that such action gave Germany a lousy name.

When I arrived in Salonika in late April 1917, Greece had two rival governments: the Venizelists in Salonika and King Constantine's government in Athens. Both sides hated each other passionately. In June 1917, the French deposed the King, and Venizelos quickly reunited the country by declaring war against the Central Powers. The Greek army fought magnificently on the Macedonian front achieving a series of stunning victories against the Bulgarians who finally capitulated in September 1918. A month later, the Ottomans surrendered.

The war finally ended and requested a long overdue vacation from the State Department. During the last four years, I couldn't return to the US due to the German submarine activity on the high seas. In November 1918, I returned to the US and was encouraged seeing the Statue of Liberty once again. I spent the next few months relaxing and catching up with family and friends before my next diplomatic appointment.

Harry Mulvaney Part 8 1919-22

After four months of blissful relaxation, it was back to the hurly-burly of diplomatic life. I was reappointed Consul-General in Smyrna, a cosmopolitan city, which I came to admire for its vibrant, precious cultural and social life. I arrived in early May with rumors circulating of an impending Greek landing.

Before I left America, I followed the proceedings of the Paris Peace Conference through the press. The Greek Premier, Eleftherios Venizelos made an excellent impression on Lloyd George, Woodrow Wilson and Georges Clemenceau delivering his nation's territorial claims. I met the Greek Premier in Salonika in 1917, who impressed me with his oratory skills and shared his nation's plans with me. He envisaged Asia Minor as the jewel in the crown for Greece.

Our Consulate was located in the European quarter behind the Smyrna quay. It was a beautiful two-story building with a lovely garden where we held our social events. Our July 4 celebration was the main social event on our diplomatic calendar. It was here that I met my future wife, Penelope Papadakis, who was the daughter of a wealthy Greek merchant in Smyrna. I was captivated by her beauty and infectious smile. Yes! Love at first sight. We got married at the Greek Church, St Photini, in November 1919, spending our brief honeymoon in Constantinople. Archbishop Chrysostomos of Smyrna performed our wedding ceremony in the traditional Greek Orthodox manner. Our beautiful daughter, Marie, was born in November 1920, bringing joy to our lives.

I became good friends with the Archbishop, who always tended to the needs of his flock. I was told his sermons were so powerful and inspiring that they could lift an individual up to heaven. He wasn't on good terms the Greek High Commissioner, Aristidis Sterghiadis, whom he regarded as a bully. One day Sterghiadis entered the church when Chrysostomos was delivering his sermon and shut down the service. The reason was that Chrysostomos criticized Sterghiadis for being pro-Turk and unsympathetic towards his own people. Unfortunately, their relationship was always frosty at best.

In my annual report of 1919, I reflected on some of the critical events of that year. Three events which would have significant consequences far beyond my tenure as Consul General. Firstly, the Greek army's occupation of Smyrna, with its attendant looting and destruction of Turkish property, angered the Turks. They wanted to rid themselves of the infidel ruling over them. Venizelos appointed Aristidis Sterghiadis as the Greek High Commissioner to administer Smyrna on behalf of the allies. The latter's brief was to ensure that all inhabitants were treated fairly and whose rights would be respected. Secondly, the Greek landing was the catalyst for Mustapha Kemal establishing his embryonic nationalist movement in Anatolia. His simple message was the liberation of his country from foreign control and domination. This appeal resonated with many former Ottoman officers and soldiers who were ready to fight under Kemal's leadership. Thirdly, the allied powers wanted to punish the Ottoman empire for its misdeeds during the First World War. The Ottoman delegation failed to persuade the allies of its case for leniency and retention of its territory. They "accepted" the loss of Arabia, Syria, Mesopotamia, and Palestine, but the Greek occupation of Smyrna hurt their national pride.

As the Greek army was achieving military victories under the command of General Leonidas Paraskevopoulos on the Asia Minor front. I became good friends with Sterghiadis, visiting him at the Greek High Commission. He returned the compliment visiting me at our Consulate. We discussed the progress of the Greek- Turkish war with its impact on Greek-Turkish relations and its more full ramifications in the Middle East. He agreed with me that Britain and France held the key to peace in this region, where they had significant economic, strategic, and diplomatic interests. Sterghiadis believed the United States had an important role to play in the establishment of peace in the Near East but chose to be isolationist instead. He lauded our institutions in the Ottoman Empire, which assisted all peoples without distinction of color, creed, religion, and race.

One day Sterghiadis brought to my attention the names of two US citizens of Greek origin from Smyrna who had been arrested for not paying their restaurant bill by the Turkish police. As American citizens, they requested to have their case heard by the US Consular Court in Smyrna. A series of treaties (known as the Capitulations) signed by European nations and the United States with the Ottoman Empire granted their foreign nationals rights and immunities from prosecution under Ottoman law. I acted as a judge and found both guilty by imposing a fine of $500. If these two had committed a capital crime, then the matter would be heard by our Minister in Constantinople.

Our daughter Marie was born around the time Venizelos lost the election to the Royalists. She had beautiful brown eyes and black hair like her mother. She gave us joy at a time when the future of the Greek presence in Asia Minor seemed doubtful. Even Greece's allies abandoned Constantine and opened the door for negotiation with Kemal. The Treaty of Sevres, which supposedly established peace between the Ottoman State and the partners, was now in tatters. Kemal's primary objective was to tear it and drive the Greeks out of Anatolia.

In the middle of 1921, the Greek army achieved a series of stunning victories with Angora ready to fall to them. They didn't anticipate that the Kemalists would fight to the death to prevent their capital from falling into Greek hands. The next 12 months would result in a stalemate between the combatants on the Asia Minor front. The Italians, French, and Russians sided with Kemal by providing him with money, munitions, and guns. On the other hand, the British tried to remain neutral, bringing her into the conflict with her French and Italian allied partners.

A cataclysm of biblical proportions was about to descend upon Smyrna. I knew things were neither good or bad for the Greek army. My feeling was that they could hold their own against the Kemalists for some time to come. How wrong I was. The Kemalists drove them out of Asia Minor. Smyrna went up in flames within a few days of the Kemalist occupation. Thousands of refugees along the Smyrna quay were crying for our help, and allied ships waited in the harbor to take their nationals. I got away in time by taking all the Consular archives with me to Piraeus. My instructions were to ensure the safety of our citizens, but humanitarian considerations triumphed. I managed to sign papers of non-Americans as American citizens saving their lives from Turkish reprisals. They all thanked me when we disembarked in Greece. Many of them went on to live in the US.

At least one good thing happened during the time of the Smyrna fire that both my wife and daughter were vacationing in the US. I was glad they were in a safe place far away from the inferno. Penelope sent a cable to our US Legation in Athens to inquire as to whether I was safe or not. Upon my arrival, I immediately replied that I got out in time before our Consulate was consumed by the raging flames. Our young daughter wouldn't have understood the magnitude of the destructive power of the fire upon this beautiful city and the suffering inflicted on innocent civilians. I would tell her the whole story when she grew up.

My last diplomatic act was appearing before our House of Representative, Committee on Immigration, to give evidence regarding the entry of Asia Minor refugees into the US. I described the holocaust that took place in Smyrna with men, women, and children crying out for help with the allies, only rescuing their nationals. I am proud of the work of our navy did assist these poor souls. One Congressman asked me, "should we let these people enter the US. Yes/No?." This individual who shall remain nameless disliked immigrants from the Balkans and the Near East. My answer was, " Yes! Yes! Yes!." but the committee decided that American citizens could sponsor their refugee relatives to enter the US so long as they met the health and residential requirements.

I wrote private letters to our relief organizations- the American Red Cross, Near East Relief, YMCA, YCW, and the Presbyterian Church praising them on the excellent work they were doing with the refugees. Their efforts showed the humanitarian spirit of what America stood for in the world. I supported President Warren Harding's public appeal to raise funds for the Asia Minor refugees and wrote letters to the editors of our American and Greek-American papers, encouraging them to contribute to the campaign. They, in turn, encouraged their readers to give generously to the president's appeal. I sent $500 but didn't want my name publicized.

I finally bowed out of the hustle-bustle of diplomatic life and became an ordinary civilian. I was free to resume my private life as a journalist, author and public speaker.

CHAPTER 4

MY CONSTANTINOPLE: PART 1

I arrived in Constantinople during the summer of 1900 from a village outside of Smyrna looking for adventure and to start a new life. My parents owned a farm where they grew figs, apricots, and dates which they sold in the huge marketplace of Smyrna. One day out of nowhere an American visited our farm inquiring about our dried fruit which he had sampled in Smyrna. "Your fruit is exquisite. I have never tasted such delicious figs and apricots in all my life", the American said. My parents were delighted to hear such an endorsement of their produce from a foreigner.

I think the American was called Robert who told us that he owned a large import/export business in San Francisco. He read about the famous Smyrna dried fruits and wished to import them to California. Robert struck a deal with my parents to import our products and was prepared to pay top dollar for it. Our family income was greatly boosted through this Godsend arrangement.

Anyway, I was lucky that I had relatives with whom I could live in the Fanar district of Constantinople. My uncle George was a prosperous merchant who provided me with comfortable quarters and three square meals a day. Before starting my employment in his business, I took the opportunity to visit many wonderful sites that is incredible city had to offer.

For the next two weeks, I spent walking every nook and cranny of this magnificent city viewing its beautiful buildings, bazaars, and religious sites. Initially, I proceeded to explore the Fanar district with its many fine wooden mansions, apartment buildings, churches, and businesses. This was the Greek heart of the city. I wanted to light a candle in the St George Cathedral only to see its doors firmly bolted. I was upset that I couldn't fulfill my religious obligation. Never mind, I found the Holy Trinity Church to light a candle and pray to the Virgin Mary. I felt relieved that I was able to make my offering. I passed outside the residence of the Patriarchate with its beautiful garden and heard young clergymen discussing matters of faith.

The next places to visit were the mosques, Taksim Square and Topkapi Palace. The Sultan Ahmed and Suleminiya Mosques were simply magnificent structures with their fine architecture and minarets rising to the sky. You could hear the hodjas from the minarets calling the faithful for prayer. Taksim Square was a huge place with Aghia Sophia in the background. I imagined the Sultan addressing his subjects that the Empire was at war with its neighbors. Suddenly, I found myself ready to enter the grounds of Topkapi Palace when two Imperial Guards stopped me. " Where do you think you're going?", one uttered in a loud voice. "I want to see its beautiful gardens," I declared. "You must leave now or else we will have to detain you." I left immediately. From this palace, the Sultan ruled his empire where he received foreign diplomats along with his cabinet ministers and businessmen.

Uncle George told me to visit the bazaars which were out of this world. He was right. The Grand Bazaar is a huge place completely undercover where one could easily get lost among the many stores with each seller vying for your business. I had never seen a place like this in my entire life. Many of the businesses were owned by Greeks, Armenians, and Jews with very few Turkish operators. You could buy anything imaginable from jewelry, gold bracelets, furniture, carpets, rugs, leather goods to clothes. Jewelry was produced in Constantinople by master craftsmen whereas carpets and rugs came from the factories of Smyrna. Some sellers sold the latest fashions from Paris and London which the rich ladies of Constantinople wore proudly.

The Spice Bazaar was an extraordinary place with its aroma of spice hitting your taste buds. You could find any spice your mind could conceive. I walked around striking up a conversation with stallholders who told me that many spices were imported from India and Egypt. Some were produced in the Empire. There were so many spice names that my mind couldn't simply remember. Momentarily, I recalled my mother's favorite dish rabbit stifado with onions, herbs, and aromatic spices. The spice bazaar and stifado made me feel very hungry. Both bazaars are simply phenomenal.

A visit to the hippodrome took me back to the glory days of the Byzantium Empire where chariot racing and social entertainment were staged. I imagined the Emperors seated in a high position where they viewed events in comfort. The arena must have been packed with thousands of spectators shouting at the top of their voices during the chariot races. I suppose there was betting on the races. This magnificent site was left to ruin with columns and walls falling into disrepair. I wondered why the Sultan didn't spend some of his largesse in restoring the hippodrome to its ancient glory.

The next place to visit was the Galata bridge built some forty years earlier linking Europe with Asia. All the foreign embassies and legations are located in the Galata district. As you walk thru here, you see foreign businesses and street signs displayed in foreign languages. One day I stopped at a Greek restaurant had lunch and became friendly with the owner. He told me that thousands of Armenians were massacred in this district over a bank robbery in 1896. It wasn't a bank robbery but Armenian heroes occupying the Ottoman Bank seeking the intervention of the European powers to save their people from massacres.

Walking across to the Asiatic side was a different world to the one found in Constantinople. The majority of the street signs and business names were written in the Ottoman script which I couldn't read. However, I found the Turks friendly who had no fear of foreigners or strangers. They made me feel welcomed.

One day, I perched myself on top of a hill overlooking Seraglio Point which spans the Golden Horn. From here I had a breathtaking view of the Bosphorus and the Marmara Sea with the Princes Islands in the distance. The Bosphorus was full of merchant ships flying foreign flags indicating the importance of Constantinople in international trade.

Before commencing work, I visited Aghia Sophia which captured my imagination of its past splendor and Byzantine mass conducted by the Patriarch thundering his sermon to his flock. This magnificent structure is a mosque that I hoped one day would return to Christianity. Only the future held the key to this realization.

Two weeks over, ready to work.

My Constantinople Part.2

After spending a few weeks of bliss visiting the wonderful sites of this magnificent city, it was time to settle into the reality of work.

Uncle George owned a large import/export business in the Fanar district where he produced beautiful handmade furniture for export to Europe and sometimes received orders from America. His furniture was renowned for its quality and received many letters from satisfied customers. He imported carpets and rugs from Smyrna which were simply exquisite and sold a variety of other goods.

He owned a large emporium where he sold his merchandise directly to the public. The majority of his clientele were wealthy and middle-class individuals who could afford to pay high prices for his goods. I was employed as a salesman but also worked in the office processing accounts when there wasn't much else to do on the sales floor. He was tough on his staff but treated us all with courtesy and respect.

My living expenses were minimal which allowed me to save money so I could open up my own business one day. We worked six ten-hour days and with Sunday our rest day. On Sunday, I went to Church to thank God for giving me good health and the opportunity to save money for my future endeavors. I never worried about shopping for food as my aunt arranged for all that. Sometimes when she was busy, she would send a servant to buy the food from the Grand and Spice Bazaars.

My daily routine varied little but there were events outside the emporium that would have a major impact on Uncle George's Emporium. The political situation in Constantinople was tense with the Empire facing major challenges from the provinces in the Balkans and Asia Minor. Macedonia was the center of this political struggle with violent clashes taking place between the Ottoman army and Bulgarian guerrillas. The Constantinopolitan newspapers published daily accounts of these events. However, the accuracy of these reports was difficult to ascertain due to the imposition of censorship in the capital.

There was a large Bulgarian community in Constantinople who went about their daily lives without stirring up Turkish passions. They seemed to be loyal citizens and never said anything about the guerrilla bands operating in Macedonia. A regular Bulgarian customer named Vladko told me that some of his relatives had been terrorized by these Bulgarian guerrilla units. In one case, they pillaged and burned his uncle's village around Florina. One of the guerrilla leaders told his uncle (Goran) that if he reported them to the Ottoman authorities, they would return and kill all of them.

When the Ottoman troops came to the village seeking information about the guerrillas, Goran told them it was the Greeks who committed this dastardly act. During this time, Greek, Bulgarian, and Serbian insurgents fought for supremacy in Macedonia with the abject goal of driving out the Ottoman Turks. Whilst their intentions seemed noble but attacking and killing innocent civilians didn't help their cause. As a Greek, I wanted Macedonia to be liberated and to come under Greek control.

The Greek press condemned the actions of these marauders who terrorized our folk in Macedonia. They reported events in a way that avoided the ire of the censor. The local Bulgarian press condemned the actions of the guerrilla bands using very strong language. Both the Greek and Bulgarian newspapers supported the Ottoman government's action in crushing these insurgents. It seemed from press reports that our Greek guerrillas "co-operated" with the Turks to crush the Bulgarian units. From what I gathered reading press reports and listening to Vladko that there was an intense hatred between the Greeks and Bulgarians in Macedonia. I thought as Orthodox Christians cooperation would have been possible to drive out the

Turks. However, this rivalry suited the Turks allowing them to drive a wedge between the warring parties.

The great European powers forced Sultan Abdul Hamid to institute political and civil reforms for his subjects in Macedonia. Nonetheless the Sultan never publicly expressed his displeasure of this external interference in his empire. The Turkish press was mute over the intervention of the European ambassadors in Constantinople. Some wealthy customers who knew members of the Ottoman Cabinet told us that the Sultan was seething over this interference in the internal affairs of Turkey.

The summer of 1908 was a momentous time with the Salonika becoming the epicenter of political change which shook the empire to its core. A group of Turkish officers (Young Turks) rebelled against the Sultan demanding the reintroduction of the 1876 Constitution that guaranteed freedom and rights to all subjects of the empire. In Constantinople, I witnessed for the first time Turks, Greeks, Bulgarians, Armenians, and Jews embracing and hugging each other with such brotherly love. That moment proved illusory. Next year, all this changed when the Young Turks espoused " Turkey for the Turks."

Despite the political turmoil, Uncle George's business performed well until 1910 with rumblings of war between Greece and Turkey. The two issues were over Crete and a spat between the Greek ambassador Gryparis and the Grand Vizier. The former was the center of Greek-Turkish relations with numerous rebellions occurred with the Cretans demanding union with Greece. These uprisings were brutally crushed by the Turks. The latter was over words uttered by the Grand Vizier which Gryparis took offense and returned to Athens for "consultation."

Meanwhile, the Sultan ordered the mobilization of the army near the Greek frontier. Athens responded in kind. I prayed that no war would eventuate. The Ottoman government ordered a Turkish boycott against Greek ships and tradesmen. This decision impacted a part of my uncle's business who depended on Greek ships for the import/export of merchandise from Greece and Europe. The Turkish press fanned its hatred towards the Greeks in Constantinople. We kept silent throughout this entire time to avoid Turkish reprisals and to be able to continue business as usual. Interestingly, the Turkish pashas continued to order their handmade furniture from uncle George. Our silence proved golden from a business perspective.

My uncle lodged a compensation claim for loss of business and surprisingly the Ottoman court accepted it without demur. Another chapter to follow soon.

My Constantinople Part 3

Thank God! war was averted between Greece and the Empire. My uncle's business continued to prosper and time had for me to go on my own. A rich pasha named Arif who came to the emporium always asked me what I wanted to do with my future. I told him I wished to open up a restaurant in the Fanar district. " I know a Greek who wants to sell his restaurant," he said. I was overjoyed when I heard his comment. Arif arranged our meeting with Vasilis Pazanoglou to discuss terms and finalize the deal. He had no ulterior motive other than wanting to help me.

Our meeting went smoothly and shook hands with the deal signed sealed and delivered. We completed all the legal formalities to commence business. I did all this in secrecy as I wasn't sure whether how my uncle would react to my decision. George envisioned that I would assume full control of his business upon his retirement since he had no heir. He was surprised when I told him and wished me all the best. That made things so much easier for me.

Commencing business before the Balkan Wars would prove interesting. The whole of Constantinople was abuzz with excitement that the Empire was ready to confront the infidel in Macedonia. I witnessed the army units marching outside my restaurant called Anatole going to the frontier. They were dressed in fine uniforms carrying the latest rifles and led by their officers on horseback.

When hostilities commenced in October 1912, I trod a fine line being Greek and an Ottoman subject. This required tact and diplomacy to avoid my restaurant being attacked by a Turkish mob. I displayed the Ottoman flag outside the restaurant as an act of loyalty towards the Empire. Many of our Turkish patrons were polite thinking that my restaurant supported the army. My conversations with the Turks never revealed my real innermost thoughts of the war. Secretly, I wanted our Greek army to smash the Turks. It worked, business boomed with many of our Turkish and Greek patrons saying that Anatole was better-managed service and menu wise compared to when Vasili owned it.

The Balkan Wars passed and peace reigned briefly. Constantinople quietened down but you could see the German presence on every street corner. I didn't like them but felt that they would cause problems for the Empire. Some well-connected Turkish customers told me that the Sultan disliked the Germans but could do nothing since the Young Turks were in bed with them. Trouble erupted sooner than expected with the assassination of Archduke Ferdinand in Sarajevo.

Europe exploded into warfare on the western front with large standing armies engaged in trench warfare. The empire remained neutral until late October 1914 when the imperial navy shelled Russian naval positions in the Black Sea. We were now at war with an Anglo-French-Russian combination. This meant that the Dardanelles would be blocked by the enemy whose sights were the occupation of Constantinople. I harbored such sentiments but avoided outwardly expressing them for business reasons.

So long as mother Greece remained neutral, we Constantinopolitan Greeks were safe from Turkish reprisals. On the other hand, we were still viewed as infidels (yiaourides) by the Turks. Displaying Turkish flags outside Greek businesses and homes showed our "loyalty" to the Ottoman state. Things could change dramatically for us if there was a change of government in Athens. The rift between Venizelos and King Constantine worried all Greeks of Constantinople. If Venizelos joined the Anglo-French side, then we faced danger but Constantine's neutrality would more beneficial for us.

When the Armenian elite was arrested in April 1915 that was a warning sign for us Ottoman Greeks. These poor souls were executed and their brethren were deported en masse into the Anatolian interior. My family in Smyrna was safe due to Governor Rahmi Bey who protected the Greeks from the Young Turk party. However, I heard from American missionaries who came to the restaurant saying that they witnessed the deportation of fellow Greeks from villages along the Black Sea. "Their treatment was indescribable", one missionary stated.

Constantinople cut-off as no railway lines was connecting the capital with Asia Minor. The Anglo-French navy ensured that no goods left Smyrna or other Ottoman ports along the Mediterranean. There were serious food shortages, life became expensive, and war-profiteering became the order of the day. People were starving. Heating fuel was available only to those who could afford to pay for it. I afforded fuel to keep the restaurant and home warm during our cold bleak winters.

Despite such difficulties, the restaurant continued to trade with a reduced menu. The patrons didn't complain knowing the situation was beyond everyone's control. I bargained with the merchants trying to buy food at a lower price than the inflated one. Sometimes I won and other times I lost. The government tried to clamp down on profiteering without any tangible success. I imagine that some government officials received bribes from merchants by turning a blind eye. Corruption was rife. I could have complained to the government but decided against it feeling they might shut down my business.

In 1917, the Ottoman newspapers were encouraging all Christians in Constantinople to enlist in the army. The press painted a positive picture of our military situation in the Near East. "Why is the press asking us to enlist when they report of military successes when I thought the opposite may be the case", I wondered to myself. Many Greeks and Armenians hid to avoid conscription. I decided to enlist in the army. Failing my medical examination was manna from heaven. Some Greeks paid Turkish doctors a fee to be declared unfit for military service.

At the recruitment office, I learned from a Turkish officer that the Greek and Armenian recruits acted as interpreters for German and Austrian officers. Some Christians were employed secretaries to Turkish officers and heads of recruiting offices. They exercised their duties loyally and were better educated than the average Turkish private.

I continued running the restaurant until the end of the war.

My Constantinople Part 4

Armistice signed October 30, 1918, war over. When I read this in our Greek press, my heart jumped for joy. The time had come to send the Sultan and his Grand Vizier packing into Asia Minor. I didn't care where he governed, so long as he never set foot again in Constantinople.

One sunny November day, I walked to the top of a hill overlooking the Golden Horn and saw ships in the far distance coming towards me. As they came into focus, I the British, French, Italian, and Greek flags blowing gently into the breeze. I felt that our wish for a Constantinople free of Ottoman rule would finally end. Of course, that would depend on what allies would decide in Paris. Seeing the Averoff with its Greek flag brought a vision of Constantinople uniting with mother Greece. The vision continued with ex-King Constantine becoming emperor of a new Byzantium. Momentarily, I thought this was all real but reality intervened.

The business started to return to "normal" with the city under allied occupation. The restaurant survived despite the continuing shortage of food, vegetables, fruit, and heating coal. Many Constantinopolitans struggled to make ends meet due to shortages and high prices. I kept our restaurant prices as low as possible to ensure our clientele kept coming back. A fine balancing act between survival and oblivion.

The local Greek press plastered the headline on their front pages "THE GREEKS ARE COMING. SMYRNA TO BECOME GREEK." Our community couldn't believe that they would witness such a momentous event in their lifetime. I couldn't believe it either. Yes! May 15, 1919, a day etched in the memory of every Greek inside and outside Greece. In the Fanar district, Greek flags were displayed on every building. You thought you were in Athens instead of Constantinople.

The remainder of 1919 was taken up with allies' indecision over the future of the Ottoman Empire and the rise of Mustapha Kemal. The latter would prove the most difficult and elusive to contain. Meanwhile, business started to pick up as the economy showed signs of improvement. Some customers started to buy the more expensive meals whereas others ate the cheaper ones. Our Turkish patrons continued to eat at our restaurant without expressing their true feelings about the allied occupation. I sensed that some Turks supported the Sultan whereas others backed Kemal. This was something the Turks needed to decide for themselves.

In early 1920, our newspapers reported Armenian massacres in Cilicia. Kemal's forces clashed with the French at Marash massacring 10,000 Armenians resulting in the allied occupation of the Ottoman War and Naval Ministries and telegraph office in Constantinople. The allies still were deciding on the fate of Ottoman Turkey. It seemed a peace treaty was still a long way off. News reports from London and Paris suggested that the Sultan would finally be removed from Constantinople. However, those Indian Moslems protested loudly to the British Government that the Sultan must remain in Constantinople. It seemed like a veiled threat to me. The British caved in to the demands of their Indian Muslim subjects.

In early March 1920 responding to the recent events in Cilicia, I invited the leaders of our local associations, societies, unions, corporations, organizations, and lodges to my restaurant to discuss the current situation in Constantinople. A heated discussion ensued with many interesting points of view expressed. Everyone believed that fortune smiled on us for Constantinople to become a Greek city. Finally, we passed a unanimous resolution pointing out that the Caliphate should be moved to Asia Minor or Arabia; Turkish guarantees were worthless and a danger to Hellas; Aghia Sophia should become a Christian Cathedral once again; international pressure to remove the Sultan and his government from Constantinople; and union with Greece.

Our resolution was handed to the Allied High Commissioners who simply forwarded it to the peace conference in London. Several of our community leaders including myself made appointments with the High Commissioners to discuss our resolution with them. You thought they all spoke from the same script. We tried to convince them that removing Sultan from Constantinople would ensure peace in Asia Minor. They simply listened, smiled, and ignored us in the end. Our request wasn't even considered by the peace conference.

A copy of the resolution was telegraphed to the Greek premier, Eleftherios Venizelos who responded that he would do his utmost to support our cause. He was a popular figure in European political circles thinking his persuasive oratory would ensure that our resolution would be presented in London. I know he tried his best but couldn't move the Anglo-French-Italian delegations supporting our position. His secretary, Sophocles Antonakis notified us that the Sultan would remain in Constantinople under certain conditions but any future breaches of the armistice would result in his expulsion.

Later in the year, I met a woman named Maria Voyatzis from Athens who came with some friends to the restaurant for dinner. She became a regular customer. There was something special that attracted me to Maria. She had a beautiful face that you could not forget. Forget I did not. Her smile and deep brown eyes sparkled in the light. Cupid's arrow pierced my heart. I couldn't wait to tell her. " Maria, I have had many sleepless nights thinking about you", I said. "What! You think about me", Maria responded with a huge smile. "Yes! Mary, I think of you constantly, I would like to get you to know better", I declared. That set off a chain of events that would change our lives forever.

In June 1921, we got married at the Holy Trinity Church in Constantinople. Her parents from Athens attended our wedding. We held the wedding reception at the restaurant inviting many friends and relatives. Everyone had an enjoyable time with plenty of food and drink that made it a memorable evening. My staff did a sterling job attending to our guests' needs. I was proud of them and rewarded with a bonus in their next pay.

We closed the restaurant for two weeks to visit our families in Smyrna and Athens. Maria loved Smyrna. She thought it was an enchanting place with its fine buildings and listening to its babble of foreign languages. Returning to Constantinople to start our life would not be without its difficulties. Events unfolding in Asia Minor would impact our local community.

My Constantinople Part 5

We started our new life with Maria who helped out in the restaurant. The business had improved significantly in the latter part of 1921. We were happy to see some old familiar faces rejoining us with their families.

Besides business, the war in Asia Minor was covered by the Greek Constantinopolitan press with huge headlines of military successes coupled with acts of bravery against determined Kemalists. I read these stories but sometimes felt the papers were hiding the real truth from us. Especially, when the Greek army failed to occupy Angora. The reversal/retreat was portrayed in glowing terms as a victory. Strange! victory. I suppose they wanted to maintain the pretense of morale and avoid problems with the military censor in Smyrna and Constantinople. I must say our local press criticized the Turks "freely" whereas the latter remained largely muted.

In early 1922, the war started looking like a lost cause which worried me about our future in Constantinople. However, this uncertainty was obviated to some extent with the presence of a strong allied occupying force who ensured our safety and security. One day this force would leave Constantinople. Our Turkish customers became more brazen towards me as the months progressed. "Your days in Constantinople are numbered, none of you giaouridis will be left," they said. I wasn't shocked by their remarks and this turnaround happened with the Greek failure to occupy Angora.

The popularity of Kemal grew in Constantinople much to the chagrin of the British and us Greeks. The French and Italians outwardly supported Kemal without any shame. Even though we had French and Italian officers coming to our restaurant, I maintained a friendly disposition towards them. It wasn't easy for me but Maria's infectious smile made our Franco/Italian customers feel at a home. Her presence boosted our business enormously.

Before the Greek attempt to occupy Constantinople in late July, Maria came towards me with a huge smile and wondered to myself what could this be. " Ready for the news", she said. "What news! What are you talking about, Maria", I replied. "We are going to be parents in early 1923", she declared. "Wow! My God this is exciting news, lets celebrate tonight", I remarked. I told our staff to stay behind after we closed as I wanted to surprise them. When I told them of our news, they were very happy for us and celebrated this with a couple of bottles of wine and mezze.

I was in a daze thinking of the wonderful event to come but the Greek defeat in Asia Minor changed all that. Mustapha Kemal was coming to eject the allies from Constantinople. That worried all the local Greeks who feared reprisals for supporting the British and the Greek army in Asia Minor. Let's not forget the Asia Minor Defence League backed by wealthy Constantinopolitan and Smyrniotes Greeks who wanted Greek control of Constantinople and Smyrna. Some of them were customers who asked me repeatedly to join them. I told them they had my moral support but that was as far I would go. The safety of my family was my prime concern.

Constantinople was overrun with thousands of refugees fleeing from Smyrna and Pontus seeking accommodation in Greece. Huge refugee camps were set up by American relief organizations on the outskirts of Constantinople to help these poor souls until the Lausanne conference decided on their future. The Kemalists wanted them removed as quickly as possible from Turkey. I feared our future in Constantinople seemed bleak and kept a low presence to avoid any troubles with the Turks.

The final peace treaty allowed Greeks who resided or arrived in Constantinople before October 30, 1918, to remain here. Anyone arriving after that date would be subject to removal under the Compulsory Exchange of Populations Convention. Maria would be a target for deportation as she was born in Athens. Our child born here could remain in Constantinople. It was an interesting situation and didn't know how this would play out. I kept quiet about it. I even asked a priest to write us a new marriage certificate showing Maria was born in Constantinople. He refused my request.

Some of our Turkish friends were supportive and could have easily reported us to the Kemalist authorities regarding Maria. They proved to be loyal friends in this case. One should never assume that all Turks are bad people. Some of them told us they disliked the Kemalists but had no choice in the matter. They preferred the last Sultan Mehmed V1 who was a gentleman according to them. I found living under the Sultan was far better than under the new administration.

The Kemalist press in Constantinople portrayed us in disparaging terms that we should all leave Turkey. I believe this press campaign was orchestrated by Angora to make us feel uneasy and fearful so we could leave voluntarily. That was unfair as I had been domiciled there since 1900. They told me we had to employ more Turks than Greeks or others if we wanted to remain in business. I didn't like it but complied with the new regulations. Turkish inspectors would come every so often to ensure we obeyed the law. Life was becoming more and more difficult under the Kemalists. I kept thinking should we remain or take the whole family to Greece. Much sleepless night was had mulling over this thought.

The Kemalists were squeezing us to leave but I thought we had protection under the exchange population convention. Then October 1924 came crashing down on my family. The Turks used

Article 2 of the Convention to force Maria, me, and our child to leave Constantinople permanently. I appealed to the Kemalists to no avail that I was an Ottoman citizen had been here since 1900 and our child was born in Constantinople. They didn't care and wanted us to leave as quickly as possible. I couldn't believe that I would be permanently severing ties with my homeland. It hurt me very much. We abandoned the restaurant and other property we owned awaiting the decision of the Mixed Commission for compensation which never came. All our hard work ended up in smoke.

We were going to Greece to start a new life with its uncertainties. Many Turkish friends who came to see us off cried as we boarded the train for Athens. I wondered what new things lay ahead for my family.

My Constantinople Part 6

We left the Orient Train State in Constantinople on November 11, 1924, and arrived 18 hours later in Athens. Maria's parents waited for us at the station and drove us to their modest home in Kifisia. They were happy to see us and followed the ordeal of the Constantinopolitan Greeks through the Athenian press. The house had three large bedrooms, a nice kitchen, and a modest front garden. I wasn't interested in gardening and wanted to work in a restaurant.

I caught the cable car near the in-law's house which took me into downtown Athens. I got off near Constitution Square and walked to Patission Street where many restaurants were located. As I walked along, I checked to see if any jobs were advertised in restaurant shop windows. This was my daily routine until the middle of 1925. Our savings gradually dwindled where they needed to be supplemented.

Meanwhile, Maria was happy to be home with her parents in Athens. Our little daughter, Christina kept her grandparents fully occupied with her skipping rope in the front garden. They swung it as she jumped and laughed to her heart's content. It brought the in-laws lots of joy playing with their only grandchild. They spoilt her to death. Christina was the center of their universe.

Finally, my job search proved successful landing work as a waiter at the Constantinople restaurant owned by a Greek named Pavlos Millarias who had come from Smyrna to Athens before the Asia Minor disaster. He was a jovial friendly individual who was impressed with my work ethic. I told him that I had owned a restaurant in Constantinople but abandoned it due to our expulsion by the Turks. Pavlos didn't know that I was born in Smyrna until after I told him. He took a liking to me calling me "patrioti." After this, we became good friends. I always maintained my professional demeanor during work time even though we were friends. Pavlos was the employer, I the employee.

Gradually we adjusted to life in Greece and our financial position improved as well. One day, I received an unexpected letter from a long-lost friend in the USA. His name, Kostas Passanoglou located me through the Greek Red Cross. In his letter, he stated that a relative had sponsored him to come to America. Kostas found life difficult at the start but quickly adapted to American ways. He went into partnership with his brother in a restaurant in Willingboro, New Jersey which was popular with the locals. We exchanged a few letters over the coming months.

In early 1926, he sent a letter that spun my head around. "Why don't you move your whole family to America, we can provide you with work and accommodation", Kostas concluded in his letter. This unexpected news needed to be discussed with Maria. I didn't know how she would react in moving across the Atlantic. She was very close to her parents. The in-laws were out so I took the opportunity to discuss it with Maria.

"I have some surprising news to tell you, I want you to listen to me carefully before you respond", I said. She sat in deep thought for a few moments before responding. " I think it's a great idea. America has more opportunities for both of us compared to living in Athens. I know you're working and have a good boss but he's not your friend. If his business doesn't do well, he will dismiss you", Maria said with a happy smile. Her positive response surprised me. I wrote back to Kostas that we found his offer appealing. Yes! We were ready to move to America. Maria's parents were shocked when I told them of our decision to leave Greece permanently. It took them a little while to accept it but accepted our decision.

Kostas sponsored us and initiated the immigration process from his end. I received a letter from the US Legation in Athens to attend an immigration interview and to do a medical examination. We passed our medical examinations with flying colors. The consular official, Michael Roberts asked me "why do you want to live in America." I paused for a moment and told him "it is a land of great opportunity and want to start a new life. I love Greece but there's no future for us here. I see the daily struggles of my fellow Asia Minor Greeks who barely survive. These were once proud self-reliant individuals who had businesses, farms, and established schools before 1922 ", I said. "Your immigration application is approved", Roberts replied.

In June 1927, our new life's adventure began crossing the Atlantic ocean bound for New York. As the ship entered New York harbor, we could see the city skyline and Ellis Island our final stop. The immigration process went smoothly. We were immigrants ready to start a new life in America. We stayed overnight in a hotel when Kostas drove us the next day to Willingboro. As we proceeded to New Jersey, I thanked him for helping us get here and also offering us accommodation and work.

Kostas and I were old school friends from Smyrna spending many summers together. We lost contact with one another before the Smyrna fire. The Greek Red Cross connected us once again. Renewing an old friendship was very important helping us to settle into our new life in America.

I worked as a waiter at Kostas's restaurant and free accommodation allowed us to save money. Occasionally we sent money to the in-laws. Despite the great recession, we survived to open up our restaurant in the town. I named it To Fanari (The Light) in memory of where I lived in Constantinople. Our American customers were intrigued by the restaurant's name. To Fanari lit the way for our success in America.

Our Greek church, St Basils was the focal point of our small community. It organized dances, sports, and cultural events including the annual picnic. Christina attended Greek school to learn our language, history, and culture. Maria became president of the Philoptochos raising money to help our poor Greek families. I never forgot Smyrna nor Constantinople but Willingboro was our new patrida.

Life is beautiful in New Jersey.

CHAPTER 5

A GUERILLA IN THE MOUNTAINS

I was born in Samsun (Amisos) on August 22, 1899, to a wealthy Greek merchant family. My father owned an import/export business dealing in carpets, rugs, and tobacco. My family also owned a farm outside the city in the nearby village of Alacam, growing fruit, and vegetables. My name is Ioannis Vogatzoglou, and this is my story.

I grew up in an affluent household in Samsun with servants to attend to all our daily needs. How lucky I consider myself to have grown up in such a family.

Most of our servants were Turks and Armenians, including a few Greeks. Our employees, whether working as servants or in our import/export business, were loyal, hardworking individuals who enjoyed working for us. Our father was a generous man who treated all his employees with respect and paid them good wages.

One day my father decided to move from the city to our farm near the beautiful village of Alacam. It was a beautiful estate where he chose to grow tobacco, which he sold on the international market. Turkish tobacco was prevalent in Europe and North America. We thought the good times would last forever.

We believed the Young Turk revolution in 1908 would usher in a new era for us Christians. My parents got caught up in the euphoria of seeing the removal of Sultan Abdul Hamid. They supported the Young Turks. How quickly things would change for us.

During the First World War, the Young Turk regime would come after us with great hatred and vengeance to kill us. First, they went for the Armenians and then began our turn. They rounded up our old men, women, and children and deported them into the Anatolian interior. Many never made it to their intended destination. They were deprived of food, water, warm clothing, and shelter. Winters were very harsh and cold, which made survival almost impossible. Very few survived their ordeal.

The lucky survivors were mere pale shadows of their former selves looking more like skeletons wearing rags instead of warm clothing. You could easily burst into eyes if you saw them. Such drama was too painful to bear. I never forgot those emaciated looking individuals who remained forever etched in my memory. By some miracle, my family escaped deportation. I could never understand this. Sometime later, I heard someone telling my father that the German Consul in Samsun used his influence with the Turkish Governor to spare our family from deportation. Whatever the reason, we're lucky at that time. At the end of the Great War, the Ottoman army demobilized and surrendered its weapons to the Allies. However, the Greek landing in Smyrna and the arrival of Mustapha Kemal in Samsoun on May 19, 1919, would complicate things for us in Pontus.

We got some relief with our Greek army winning several battles on the Asia Minor front during 1920. We felt secure and rest assured that we continue to live in our ancestral homeland despite the Kemalist threat.

However, the change of government in Athens in November 1920 raised concern for us since the allies wanted to open dialogue with the Kemalists. The Greek navy made the situation worse by shelling several coastal cities in Sinope, Samsun, and Trebizond in the middle of 1921. All the Kemalists needed an excuse to commence deportations of our people into the Anatolian interior. We were hoping that our Greek army would occupy Angora. It failed in its mission, which meant that we had no future in Pontus.

I remember the horrible butcher Topal Osman and his cutthroat chettes (guerillas). His men raided our village by burning, killing, and plundering the personal wealth and property of our villagers. The beautiful young women were sent to Turkish harems, and Turkish families adopted young children. They killed all our young men. Some older men, women, and children deported into the Anatolian interior who never seen again.

His men entered our house, killing everyone in sight and finally torching our house. My parents, who spoke Turkish, appealed to Osman's men to let them go, but they murdered them in cold blood, including my siblings. I was lucky to escape as I hid in the basement of our home. Lucky for me, they didn't search there.

Those of us who luckily survived escaped to the Pontic mountains and joined our Greek guerilla brothers. I chose survival over dying. Osman's chettes and the Kemalist army were ambushed at every opportunity. The Bolsheviks supplied the Kemalists with money and weapons. We replenished our depleted arsenal from captured Russian weapons. We tried to make their lives as difficult as possible to help our Greek army remain in Asia Minor.

In early 1922, the Kemalist Interior Minister, Fethi Bey, launched a surprise attack on us trying to flush us out. We fought heroically against a superior force and finally managed to repulse them. Turkish losses were high compared to ours. We were determined to survive at all costs and knew if captured, they would kill us.

Our life in the mountains was hard, but we always had enough food and water to survive the harsh conditions. We never remained in the same spot and kept the Turks guessing as to our whereabouts. We gathered around the warm campfire and discussed the good times we once enjoyed and also what would be the fate of our people in Turkey. We entertained ourselves through our Pontian dances and singing some of our traditional songs. We felt very proud of being Pontian Greek.

We survived in the Pontic mountains until the end of the Greek-Turkish war in September 1922. We surrendered to the Kemalists, who oppressed us. They executed some of our fellow fighters for treason against the Kemalist state. I was lucky to escape execution and ended up as a refugee in Greece in 1924.

CHAPTER 6

A TURK TELLS HIS STORY

My name is Ahmet Kaner, and remember the days of May 1919 and September 1922 as though they happened yesterday. I am now 90 years old telling my children, grand and great children, what happened on those momentous days when I was growing up in Izmir. In those days, it was known as Smyrna.

My father, Faizal, and mother, Fatma, were kind, humble, and gentlefolk who never hated anyone. We lived in the Turkish Quarter of the city, where we had some Greek neighbors. I think their family name was Menidis. Our families got on well with each other. There were times when my parents invited the Menidis family for lunch and sometimes for dinner. The Menidis's reciprocated.

I played with their children and remembered the great times we shared. As children, we didn't know or understand the politics that was unfolding between our Ottoman Government and our neighbors. These were innocent years for us. We didn't care about politics, all we knew was playing our games in front of our houses. How we loved playing hopscotch and hide and seek.

When the First World War broke out, I was 10 years old and remembered my father enlisting to fight for our country. I remember his letters sent from the various war fronts. Mother would read his messages to me as to what he saw during the battles with our enemies. Father got wounded in some action in the Middle East and came home to recover from his wounds in a military hospital in Izmir. He never saw combat again. For my mother and me, we were over the moon that he had been discharged from the army.

My father blamed the Young Turks, especially Enver and Talaat, for landing us in a war that we should have never participated in. Many of our people died for these terrible creatures. Father disliked the Germans who had too much influence in our Empire. He found them arrogant and treated us as if we were their lackeys. Furthermore, my parents strongly disapproved of the deportation of our Armenian and Greek citizens. They were afraid to speak up, fearing they would be killed by our authorities. Their silence was golden.

I was now 14 years old at the end of the war and glad it was all over. We suffered from food shortages, lack of heating coal, and medicines. My father resumed his work as a clerk in a large Greek department, Missailidis Brothers, along the Smyrna quay. His employer valued him as an employee and promoted him to chief purchasing officer. Father purchased the latest Paris fashions from major French suppliers in Paris, Lyons, and Marseilles. His knowledge of Greek, Armenian, and English was highly valued by his employer.

In May 1919, Izmir Turkish newspapers reported rumors that the Greek army was to take over our city. My father was horrified at the prospect of seeing our former enemy taking control. I remember father saying it was the war that brought out his lousy blood towards Greece. Anyway, he couldn't do anything about it. He carried on doing his work and minded his own business.

Then rumors of a Greek landing proved right. It was a day of celebration for the local Greeks, whereas sadness descended like a dark cloud upon us. I remember hearing shots ringing out as the Greek army marched down the main street of Izmir. All hell broke loose as Turkish businesses and properties were looted and destroyed by our local Greek compatriots. Some of our Turkish friends were killed in this horrible episode. No one ever found out who fired the first shot.

The Greeks appointed Aristidis Sterghiades as its High Commissioner in Izmir. He took swift action by jailing and hanging his Greek compatriots who had destroyed Turkish property or had killed Turks. With tensions running high between us Turks and the Greeks, Sterghiades action quietened down the situation. People were able to go about their business unmolested.

I remember my father feeling outraged as to what happened to us at the time of the Greek landing. Our relations with the Menidis family became cool and stopped seeing each other for a time. As the situation improved in Izmir, my parents began to reach out to them. Things between our two families gradually grew. It was like old times. Little did I know that in 12 months that our relations with the Menidis family would be severed forever.

The Greek army's failure to occupy Ankara (Angora) in September 1921 was the turning point in our war with the Greeks. My father wasn't too keen on Mustapha Kemal, whom he considered a rebel and a traitor to our Sultan Mehmed V1. Our government in Istanbul was doing its utmost to establish peace, security, and prosperity in our war-torn country. Everyone was war-weary and wanted things to get back to normal.

In September 1922, the Greek army suffered a catastrophic defeat, including the departure of thousands of Greek refugees to Greece. I was 18 years old when I saw the thousands of refugees waiting to be rescued along the Izmir quay. I didn't believe that our Greek citizens would leave in such terrible circumstances. They weren't even allowed to take more of their possessions with them.

On September 13, a fire broke out in the Armenian Quarter, which quickly spread to other parts of Izmir. My parents worried about the Menidis family and other Greek neighbors for their safety. I went to our Greek neighbors' houses, checking to see if they were inside. In the chaos and confusion raging in Izmir, I managed to get them to stay with us until we could get them out of Turkey.

Our house was spared from the fire. The Kemalists knocked on every door in our street, checking to see if we were harboring any Greeks or Armenians. We had a cellar in our house, which we hid our neighbors. Luckily, the Kemalists missed it. We managed to smuggle them to safety, disguising them as Americans. How they weren't molested or stopped by the Kemalists was the gracious, merciful hand of Allah.

My parents and I were unfortunate to see the Menidis family leave in such circumstances. Despite troubles between Greece and Turkey, my family loved and respected the Menidis's. We cried and embraced one another as brothers and sisters never to cross our paths again.

The moral of the story is that people should love and forgive each other. War brings hatred and death. I hope the children of Menidis think the same way I do. Let peace reign in our hearts.

CHAPTER 7

AN AMERICAN RELIEF WORKER REMEMBERS

M y name is Ebenezer Robertson, an American relief worker working for the Near East Relief (NER) organization. I was born to American parents (Robert and Elizabeth Robertson) in Constantinople in May 1900. Both my parents were born into well-off families in Boston towards the end of 1865. They were imbued with the Christian zeal to help less fortunate people and to convert them to Christianity. Coming to Ottoman, Turkey posed a challenge for them working in a Muslim society. They stuck to their primary task of engaging with non-Muslims without proselytizing the Turks.

My parents came to the Ottoman Empire in late 1894. They were sent by the American Board of Commissioners for Foreign Missions (ABCFM) in Boston to conduct missionary work amongst the Armenians and Greeks in Asia Minor. They arrived in Constantinople in the early stages of the Hamidian massacres against the Armenians. The ABCFM was active in the Ottoman Empire for almost a century.

My mother was a school teacher teaching English to Armenian, Greek, and Turkish children in an American school in Constantinople. Father traveled across Asia Minor, visiting our missionary schools and hospitals to ensure that they discharged their duties efficiently and sent his reports back to Boston. My mother retired from teaching at the end of the Great War, and my father continued with his relief work until December 1919. Both of them returned to the US in early 1920.

I grew up in the multiethnic district of Pera hearing a babble of foreign languages: Greek, Armenian, Turkish, German, Italian, and Danish. It was an exciting time growing up and playing with children of different ethnic, cultural, and religious backgrounds. Most of my friends were Greeks, Armenians, and Turks. These three groups got on well together until the outbreak of the Balkan and First World Wars. Then, things changed with massacres taking place, first the Armenians and later the Greeks. It was painful seeing once Turkish friends and neighbors learning to hate their Armenian and Greek compatriots with a passion. I blame extreme nationalism and religious fanaticism as the main culprits that drowned Asia Minor in blood.

Every summer, our family would vacation in the USA. I had an excellent opportunity to become acquainted with my parent's families. I would go swimming with my cousins to a lake outside of Boston. We had plenty of fun. Other times, we went on family picnics to the countryside where I played games with my cousins. These were cherished moments in my life. At the end of summer, we went by train to New York to catch the boat for Constantinople. Our sea journeys were usually comfortable and pleasant with the occasional sea storm. The ABCFM always paid our return fares.

When war broke out in Europe in early August 1914, we were vacationing in the USA. Since Turkey remained neutral, my parents decided to return to Constantinople due to their work commitments. We arrived in early September and ready for another school year. When Turkey entered the war in October of that year, things changed for the Europeans. Many packed their bags and left. The Turks didn't molest

Americans. However, when we severed our diplomatic relations with Turkey in April 1917. It was time for us to leave. We went to Salonika for the remainder of the war, where my parents remain inactive for some 18 months. Life in Salonika was not easy for us.

The one thing I remember was the great fire of Salonika in August 1917. It destroyed a lot of houses with the fire starting along the waterfront and spreading out into the neighborhoods. The flames did not spare commercial buildings, banks, restaurants, schools, and religious institutions. By some miracle, we escaped the inferno but saddened to see so many homeless people. Some neighborhoods and ancient sites survived as the flames danced along their periphery.

My parents returned to Constantinople in early 1919, with my father working as a relief worker with the American Committee for Relief in the Near East (ACRNE). His task was to help the thousands of Armenian, Russian, and Greek refugees that overran Constantinople. These individuals need to be fed, clothed and provided with medical care. He discharged his duties like a good Christian towards the refugees. I got involved with relief work as well. My mother stayed home taking care of our household. Finally, my parents returned to America for good.

I stayed behind to carry out relief work for the ACRNE (later renamed Near East Relief) in the Caucasus and Constantinople. I enjoyed every moment helping these unfortunate refugees who many had no country to go. They depended on American aid for their survival. Our NER personnel were scattered far and wide in Asia Minor, doing their best to assist people without distinction of race and religion.

All of a sudden, Smyrna became the center of press attention. The defeat of the Greek army and its occupation by the Kemalists. Smyrna was full of thousands of refugees seeking to escape to safety, which many were perishing in the terrible fire which started in the Armenian quarter. The fire spread to other parts of Smyrna, leaving a once cosmopolitan city reduced to an ash heap.

The refugees were arriving by the boatload to Piraeus, Salonika, and the Greek islands. The worst humanitarian disaster in the annals of human history. Greece was overrun by this mass of humanity that needed to be fed, clothed, housed, and provided with medical care. The NER would take up the challenge to assist the refugees. Not an easy task, but donations from the American public alleviated some of the distress of these poor wretched souls.

I was assigned to work in two refugee camps in the Athens area. The first camp was located at the foot of the acropolis near the Parthenon. Imagine the seat of democracy reduced to a sea of tents housing some 5,000 refugees, mainly women, children, and elderly folks. These people had very few personal possessions, just the clothes on their backs. Unfortunately, some of the elderly and women died due to insufficient medicines from typhoid, malnutrition, and tuberculosis. Some orphan children needed help. After eight months, they moved me to a place called Kokkinia to continue my relief work. In September 1923, I returned to America and campaigned actively to raise funds for the orphans. I spoke to various community groups in Boston, New York, and Chicago about the plight of these children. The generosity shown by people was touching and raised over twenty thousand dollars for our orphanage in Athens. I returned to Athens in early 1924 and had discussions with the Greek government regarding the orphans.

My negotiations with the Greek government focused on the question of finding suitable accommodation for the orphans. They couldn't be left roaming the streets by themselves or living in tents. The Greek Minister of Welfare, Kostas Danopoulos, mentioned a couple of locations that might be suitable for the establishment of our orphanage. I inspected them, but none suited our purpose.

I found an abandoned building near the center of Athens, which became our orphanage with American money. The building didn't need much renovation. At last, the children had a permanent place to sleep, eat, and play rather than living in tents or being moved around from place to place. They seemed happier, playful, healthy, and also receiving an education. They never received school education in the refugee camps. The President of the Hellenic Republic conferred the medal of Phoenix for my humanitarian work with the refugees. I returned to America in late 1923 to take up a senior position with the NER.

I returned to Athens in December 1925 to see how our orphanage operated. I was amazed at the progress we had achieved with the orphans. Our sole mission was to teach the orphans to be self-supporting and not depend on welfare. Some boys who learned carpentry went on to become successful builders. Our girls learned sewing, cooking, and embroidery, which prepared them for home duties.

In 1930, I became the Director of NER.

CHAPTER 8

AN ORPHAN TELLS HER STORY

I decided to write down my life story for my children and grandchildren in 1999. My name is Aliki Swann, and I was born to Greek parents (Eleftherios and Maria Mastoris) in Constantinople in May 1910. My father was a successful businessman who often traveled to Athens for business. He was a master tailor-making suits and pants for the Ottoman elite and wealthy Greeks and Armenians. Besides tailoring, he sold locally and imported made clothing at his department store in Constantinople. My mother ran the household and raised us five children. I had two brothers (Alexandros and Haralambos) and two sisters (Evdokia and Lana) who were older than me.

When Turkey entered the war in October 1914, my father was on a business trip to Athens. He decided to remain there to avoid conscription in the Ottoman army. He opened up a branch in Athens, which allowed him to survive there. My father was a prosperous tailor, making suits and pants for the wealthy classes. His customers were delighted with the quality of his work. He wired money to the family in Constantinople whenever he could.

At the start of hostilities, money was sent via Western Union in Athens to its branch in Constantinople. When Turkey severed its links with the United States in April 1917, he managed to send money via a Swiss company. My mother would receive a phone call from them to go to pick it up. Our father was a good provider despite his absence.

Eleftherios had a passing interest in Greek politics but stuck to his business without revealing his political leanings. My father was angry over the Royalist government's decision to allow a German-Bulgarian force to occupy Greek soil in June 1916. However, he plodded on with his business until Eleftherios Venizelos established his provisional administration in Salonika in opposition to King Constantine's government in Athens.

He enlisted with the Venizelists and fought against the Bulgarians on the Salonika front. He died from his wounds in early 1918. My mother went into a deep depression learning of his death. I believe my mother received the sad news via the Spanish Embassy in Constantinople. She never recovered and died of a broken heart in early January 1921.

I remember mother telling us of the difficulties of daily life in Constantinople during the war. We faced shortages of food, heating coal, and high prices. The money our father sent helped us to survive somehow. Within a space of a few years, all my siblings died, making me an orphan. I didn't have any relatives to take of me or knew of any until I came to live in America.

I later learned that my father had a major disagreement with his two brothers (Socrates and Nikolaos) over some business deal. I never found out the nature of their dispute, nor do I care. My father became closer to the mother's side of the family. Our maternal grandparents loved him like he was their own son. We never played with our cousins on the father's side of the family in Constantinople. One of his brothers, Uncle Socrates, went to live in America in 1913.

I wandered through the streets of Constantinople, begging to survive. Some people gave me food, and others threw a coin or two into my begging bowl. One day I came across a Greek orphanage called Agia Varvara run by Greek nuns. I knocked on the door, and this nun took me inside. She was sympathetic to me. This orphanage was also receiving financial support from the Near East Relief (NER) organization. Some 100 orphans were living here who looked well-fed, well-clothed, and happy. It put a smile on my face, Little did I know that my life was to change in the coming months.

In the middle of 1921, Mrs. Florence Johnson, a prominent socialite from New York City, visited our orphanage. She was part of a mission to make a movie about the activities of the field stations and orphanages run by the NER in Constantinople and other regions in Asia Minor and the Caucasus. The idea behind the film was to raise public awareness and solicit donations from the American public. Mrs. Johnson took a liking to me from the outset.

I played a young American girl in the film Alice in Starvingland. The plot involved a young girl named Alice who stowed away on a ship for Constantinople. There she meets her father, a NER worker, where both embarked on tours of NER orphanages and relief stations in Turkey and the Caucasus. Young Alice met healthy orphans who entertained her with Greek and Armenian songs. She was saddened to see orphans denied admission into the US. Alice understood it was impossible to care for every orphan and was inspired to assist them upon her return to America.

Florence Johnson liked me so much that she adopted me as her daughter. My Uncle Socrates Peropidis (my father's brother) challenged my adoption in a New York City court. I believe he changed his name as he wanted nothing more to do with the Mastoris side of the family. He tried everything to have my adoption overturned, but Florence fought him tooth and nail to keep me. In the end, the judge asked me whom I wanted to live. " I want to live with Florence," I said. Poor! Uncle Socrates, he was distraught with my decision. Nevertheless, we became good friends and visited his family as often as possible. Imagine my lack of contact with my cousins in Constantinople was achieved in the new world.

The film was screened in New York City, Manchester (New Hampshire), Boston, and Washington DC on December 20, 1921, and 1922. I had the opportunity, along with Florence, to visit many towns and cities on the east coast to promote the film. The actors portrayed in the movie were the orphans themselves.

Church organizations screened the film helping to raise money for the NER. The film proved an outstanding success with school children, and adults were seeing the work of the NER in Asia Minor and the Caucasus. It inspired Americans old and young to donate money to this worthy cause. I was so happy that I contributed to helping out the orphans.

My school attendance was interrupted as we traveled around the country for the NER, and later the Near East Foundation (NEF) raising funds through bazaars and serving Greek coffee. I met this wonderful young girl, Debora Zaimi, who graduated from a NEF school in Tirana, Albania, who came to America and lived with us for a while. We became very close friends until her death in 1956.

I completed high school and enrolled at Allegany University in Lexington, Kentucky, in 1930. I graduated with a degree in English and Greek literature, which I thoroughly enjoyed. A local high school in Lexington was seeking an English teacher for its 7-8th grades. I immediately applied for the position and was told to come for an interview. They offered me the job which I gladly accepted.

I met my future husband, John L.Swann, a dance instructor at Arthur Murray studios while holidaying in New York in the summer of 1937. I resigned from my position at Lexington High School and moved to New York, taking up a new job at Astoria High in the fall of 1937. We courted for the next 18 months or so and finally got married on September 20, 1939. We had two daughters whom I taught them to care about orphans and the least fortunate in our society. Most of what I taught them came from the fictional character, Alice in Starvingland. I am proud to state that my daughters have followed in my footsteps working and raising money for the NEF.

I received a medal from the NEF for my contribution to the organization in May 2000. It felt marvelous to receive such an honor.

CHAPTER 9

MY LAST DAYS IN SMYRNA, SEPTEMBER 1922

I am recounting my experience living in Smyrna before its occupation and destruction by the Kemalists in September 1922. I was lucky to be alive and thanks to the actions of a kind American, John Burgess, who saved my life. He helped me come to America and adopted me as his son.

I was born in September 1908 into a wealthy Greek family in Smyrna, where my father, Alexandros Konstantinidis, owned a large department somewhere near the quay. Our department store sold clothing, shoes, furniture and a variety of other goods which I can't recall. Many of the ladies bought the latest Paris fashions, which father imported from France. Most of our women customers were typically Greek, Armenian, or Levantine, who were financially well off. We had very few Turkish women customers. I could never figure out why we never had more Turkish customers since our staff was multilingual.

We lived in Bournava, a wealthy suburb of Smyrna, where many affluent Greek families resided. We had a large house with many rooms and an exquisite garden. My parents frequently held big lavish parties. These were grand times playing with children of other wealthy Greek families. Sometimes we would gather around the piano to listen to my mother play some beautiful songs. We all joined in the singalong. Our beautiful angelic voices brightened up our day. I thought the good times would last forever.

My last three months in Smyrna were full of surprises. I didn't know what was brewing below the surface. I remember hearing my father discussing political events with his businessmen friends at the Greek club. Occasionally he took me along with him to the Greek club where I sat in the corner, minding my own business. I didn't realize that these events would come crashing down on us in the weeks ahead.

I read the local Greek newspapers and must confess that I didn't understand all the news stories of what was unfolding on the Asia Minor front. I asked my father to explain what did it all mean. He reassured me that everything was fine. As a young boy, I trusted his word. Mother was not interested in politics and ensured the smooth running of our household. We had servants who cooked, cleaned, and maintained our large garden.

Many years later, I wanted to find out the truth about the destruction of my beautiful Smyrna. In late July 1922, King Constantine threatened to occupy Constantinople as a means of ending the conflict in Asia Minor. He never went through with his action and could have quickly conquered the city. The British threatened to shell Piraeus, and Constantine immediately backed down. Constantinople was there for the taking. A missed opportunity for glorious Constantinople to be united with Greece. Our Greek army and our national finances were in a terrible state. We always believed that we would remain in Asia Minor for a long time. Of course, that never happened.

After the Constantinople fiasco, we learned about the autonomy of Smyrna through our high commissioner, Aristidis Sterghiadis. He made his proclamation to a large crowd composed of Greeks,

Armenians, Jews, and Circassians who had gathered outside the high commission building. The declaration was well received by the attendees. However, the vast majority of Turks were horrified that Smyrna would eventually become a part of Greece. A small number of Turks were pleased with the Greek administration and loathed Mustapha Kemal, whom they regarded as a rebel and traitor to the Sultan in Constantinople.

We were told that we had a sufficient number of troops and weapons to defend and protect our province from a Kemalist attack. Apparently, funds would be pouring from wealthy Greeks living in America, England, and Egypt to bankroll the new autonomous region. Of course, the establishment of the autonomous zone was the brainchild of the Asia Minor Defence League, who wanted nothing to do with Greece under Constantine. The Asia Minor Defence League strongly believed in the viability and survival of this new entity under the dominion of the Sultan.

What did this all mean? The Greek government abandoned us and wanted to get out of Asia Minor. We would be left to fend for ourselves and one primary reason why many Smyrniotes hated Constantine. Yes! We were left to hang dry by the Greek royalists.

Several days later, we read in the local Greek press of Lloyd George's speech to the House of Commons supporting our interests in Asia Minor. I remember my father's delight thinking that the British prime minister would do everything in his power to support our cause. Maybe Lloyd George wanted to help us but had to contend with other members of his cabinet who supported the Turks instead of us.

I recall seeing people marching down the main streets of Smyrna carrying a massive banner with an inscription "HURRAY LLOYD GEORGE." The Greeks and Armenians were proud supporters of Lloyd George and his close friend, Eleftherios Venizelos. These two were seen as heroes who had liberated us from the Ottoman yoke. The situation in Smyrna was still excellent, but dark clouds were gathering in the depths of Asia Minor. It unleashed a storm, which was something none of us ever expected.

All of a sudden, our army collapsed in Asia Minor, and within days the Kemalists rode into Smyrna in an orderly fashion. They told us we had nothing to fear, and our safety would be guaranteed. That was a lie.

My parents' house was burned to the ground by Turkish guerillas (chetes). I don't recall how they managed to reach the Smyrna quay in the hope of escaping to Greece. We huddled together, along with thousands of others waiting to be rescued by our allied friends. There was a raging inferno at our backs, which scared all of us. Suddenly, Turkish soldiers came while we're standing on the quay and took both my parents away. My father tried to explain to them in Turkish that we were loyal Ottoman citizens. His protests fell on deaf ears. One of the Turkish soldiers hit him with his rifle butt in the stomach. Father fell to the ground, and another soldier said to him, "get up, you dog." As he got up, he was called a "yiaour" (infidel). Mother was assaulted by the soldiers. Tears streamed down my checks and not realizing that I would never see my parents ever again. I don't know how long they survived and how they perished in their captor's hands.

I wondered whether I would perish or survive. An American college professor who was about to board a U.S motor launch to take him to one of the US naval ships in the harbor saw me crying. He immediately came over and said, " come with me" in Greek. He told the American sailor that I was a US citizen and boarded the ship bound for Piraeus. On arrival, he took me to the US legation in Athens and told them that I was his nephew and had lost my passport in the Smyrna fire.

At the legation, they asked me if I spoke English and replied, "yes." After receiving my U.S passport, we sailed for New York and never imagined four months earlier that I would end up living in America. John Burgess allowed me to retain my Greek name and helped me start a new life.

CHAPTER 10

A CAPTAIN REMEMBERS SEPTEMBER 1922

I am telling my family of an event that I experienced as the captain of the Japanese freighter, Tokei Maru, in the harbor of Smyrna, Turkey, on September 14-15, 1922. My name is Lou Sato, and I was 35 years old at the time. It is an event that I will never forget as long as I live.

The Nippon Yusen Kaisha shipping line based in Yokahama, Japan, owned the Tokei Maru. Our company-owned a large number of merchant ships that traveled to Europe, the US, and Australia. We were the largest shipping company in Japan. We competed for cargoes against major British, French, Italian, and American companies in northern European waters, Mediterranean and Black Seas.

Our journey started in Yokohama, stopping in Hong Kong, Singapore, Aden, Suez Canal, Smyrna, Marseilles, London, and Liverpool loading and unloading cargoes in these ports. We followed the same route back to Yokohama.

We were somewhere between Marseilles and Smyrna when our radio operator picked up a wireless message to go to Smyrna urgently. Something major was happening there. When I received this message,

I immediately wired our Smyrna agent to seek confirmation of it. " Come quickly, the city is thronged with thousands of refugees waiting to be rescued, "was the reply from our agent.

I sent another message asking for further details of what was happening in Smyrna. Our agent didn't give me any details but said: "just get here as quickly as possible." I was somewhat puzzled why he didn't report the actual situation. Sometime later, I learned that he was a Greek named Stefanos and was afraid to tell us the real story fearing that the Turks might arrest him.

We were some 24 hours away from Smyrna and instructed our crew to make haste to that port. The crew responded magnificently to my call. The sea was calm with a beautiful blue sky. I could not conceive in my mind the awful scenes that we were to face as we entered the harbor of Smyrna.

I could see lots of smoke in the distance as we were approaching Smyrna. The flames were black with some red in it as it reached the sky. One of my crew said that it reminded him of Dante's inferno. The fire was like hell on earth. I could not believe that this beautiful city where I stopped previously was being reduced to ashes.

We arrived at 2 pm on September 14. We were horrified seeing all these unfortunate souls thronged along the quay waiting to be rescued. These poor souls had a raging inferno at their backs. I saw French and Italian warships in the harbor rescuing their nationals. In contrast, the Americans and the British did their best to take refugees. I was highly critical of the actions of the French and Italians. In contrast, I gave kudos to the American and British responses.

Our ship finally berthed along the quay. I went to see our agent and told him about my plan of action. Stefanos was horrified that I would be ditching our expensive cargo into the sea. " Are you mad?" he said. " I am not mad. It is about helping innocent people who are potentially facing death," I said. I wasn't concerned about my expensive cargo. I was more interested in doing a humanitarian act, saving some of these lives. After my encounter with Stefanos, I visited a Turkish officer named Colonel Ahmet Bey to see what I could do for these wretched individuals.

He received me at his military headquarters showing a friendly disposition and speaking politely to me. When I raised the issue of refugees, he went into a rage shouting that these infidels were traitors and would not be released at all. I appealed to him in the name of humanity that these individuals should be released into my care. " I would take full responsibility for their welfare and evacuation," I retorted.

Colonel Ahmet's response was an emphatic, "NO." I tried to appeal to his good nature. He remained unfazed by my plea. I again pleaded with him to release the refugees, and this time, he insulted our Japanese flag. Insulting our flag was unforgivable. I immediately demanded a formal apology from Colonel Ahmet and told him that failing this, I would summon the intervention of our Japanese High Commissioner, Count Uchida, in Constantinople.

He didn't want a diplomatic incident and conferred with his superiors regarding the release of the refugees into my care. The Turk needed allies and wanted to be seen as not wholly heartless in their negotiations with their recent enemies. They never offered a formal apology to Japan but were merely happy to see these refugees leave Turkey.

We took 825 refugees, including Stefanos from Smyrna, to Piraeus, Greece. Yes! I ditched our cargo into the harbor, thinking that saving innocent lives were worth more than our expensive merchandise. My crew displayed great humanity tendering to the needs of these people. I remember many of them telling us how happy they were to have been rescued by the Japanese. Some of the refugees thought our act of saving them was heroic.

We arrived in Piraeus. The harbor was full of ships with refugees who hadn't been processed by the Greek authorities. Some of the Athenian newspapers reported of our rescue story and stay in Piraeus. We stayed four days before embarking on the return journey to Yokohama.

I took the opportunity to catch the train for Athens. On my arrival, I walked around the city, seeing tents at the bottom of the Acropolis to accommodate the refugees. The town faced a population explosion, a human-made crisis unparalleled in the annals of history. The refugees brought very few personal possessions with them. It was sad seeing young children crying and hungry.

The events of September 1922 in the harbor of Smyrna were never erased from my memory.

CHAPTER 11

A CHILD'S TOUR TO GREECE

I am writing my story some forty years after the event describing my experience as a child witnessing the plight of Greek refugees in 1924. It is intended for my grandchildren to use their privileged position to assist the poorest members of our society. I encourage them to organize fundraising for refugees displaced by conflict. We have a moral responsibility to do something to assist the destitute and those displaced by war. Being rich and privileged did not guarantee continued financial success and enjoying the good life. An individual could lose all their wealth and end up like the Greek refugees. Nothing is guaranteed in this life.

My father John McWeather was a very wealthy industrialist and philanthropist in Trenton, New Jersey. He owned and operated several businesses producing household furniture and steel. Also owned several coal mines in Tennessee, West Virginia, and Wyoming. These mines were very lucrative for my father's business.

One day he read in the newspaper about the plight of refugees who went by boatload to Greece at the end of the Greek-Turkish war. He was shocked to see photos of men, women, and children wearing rags for clothes. They had very few worldly possessions with them. They had left their houses, properties, businesses, and farms in Asia Minor. The refugees could no longer return to their homes. They were forced by circumstances beyond their control to start new lives in an alien country. Even though they were Greeks from Asia Minor, the local Greeks called them "Turks" and told them "Go back from where you came from."

John was so moved by the plight of these refugees that he decided to help them. My father was well-known in business and political circles. He contacted some of his business friends to form a committee to raise money for Near East Relief, the American Red Cross, and the Young Men's Christian Association. His committee launched a public appeal to raise money for these destitute people. He donated $50,000 towards this appeal. I also participated in fundraising at my school. The public was asked to donate clothing, blankets, shoes, furniture, and tinned food besides money. His committee raised well over three million dollars which was then donated to our charitable organization.

The Near East Relief was so impressed with John's fundraising effort that they asked him whether I could go to Greece to hand over a check to our relief organizations. By the way, my name is Ralph, I lived a privileged life surrounded by servants and nannies. I had no idea what it meant to be poor or see refugees wearing rags. Finally, John gave his permission to the Near East Relief for me to travel to Greece. I was twelve years old in 1924.

We left New York harbor onboard the Atlantic Queen with the weather being very kind to us all the way until our disembarkation in Piraeus. I remember a car was waiting to take us to our hotel in Athens. The streets from Piraeus to Athens were thronged with many people waiting to get a glimpse of me. The Greek people greeted me like royalty. Such enthusiasm expressed by the people remained with me for the rest of my life. Unforgettable memories.

I wondered to myself why I received such a great reception in Greece. The Near East Relief and my father's committee issued a press release in all major American newspapers stating that I was going to Greece. This press release was published in all Athenian newspapers which caught the imagination of Athenians. A young child was coming from the other side of the world to see refugees and hand over a check. Even before we left New York, the Greeks knew about my coming to their beautiful country.

The Near East Relief filmed my trip to Greece and had it played in movie theaters throughout America. This was a promotional film titled Ralphy Goes to Greece showing our public that their money and other contributions (clothing, shoes, etc) were helping the refugees. It greatly assisted the fundraising effort. Unfortunately, our government did not lift a finger to help the refugees. They were more interested in doing business with Turkey and also had their sights on the rich oilfields of Mosul in Iraq. Our government was interested in helping our businesses to find new trading opportunities in Greece.

We arrived at the Great Bretagne Hotel and stayed on the third floor. From there, we could see the Akropolis from our balcony. The next morning, a car picked us up from the hotel and took us to a refugee camp beneath the Parthenon. The multitude of tents were the homes of the refugees who lived in squalid conditions. A scene of misery, destituteness, and hopelessness was etched in the faces of these refugees. I burst into tears seeing fellow children having no shoes and eating dry bread. I could see myself as a child of privilege in America. Our American organizations were doing their utmost to assist in the survival of these refugees. Many of these destitute souls would have perished without our aid. Our second day in Greece was over.

Our third day was full of surprises. There was a large crowd to greet us outside a large building known as the Zappeion Megaro situated in the center of Athens. A large palatial structure is used for meetings, exhibitions, and ceremonies. It had a large circular courtyard surrounded by Greek marble columns. An impressive structure that was worthy of the Olympian Gods. We were taken to the large courtyard where we met the Archbishop of the Greek Church, the Greek President and Prime Ministers, high-ranking officers of the Greek army, and the well-to-do of Athenian society. As we entered the courtyard, the Greeks and Americans were draped off one of the columns. The Near East Relief logo was also proudly displayed alongside the two national flags. I was seated in between the Archbishop and the President and witnessed different Greek dances and heard the recitation of Greek poetry. I did not understand a word of Greek but sensed the poetry had powerful messages.

The Greek and American national anthems were played before the commencement of this cultural event. I stood proudly to both anthems. A young Greek boy dressed in national costume sang the words of the national anthem. After the playing of the anthems, the Archbishop made a speech and blessed the success of the event. We were treated to a variety of Greek dances performed by orphan children from the island of Syros. Some children were dressed in Greek national costume whereas others wore raggedy clothes. Apparently, some dances originated in Asia Minor. I forget the names of these dances. One thing, they were lively and entertaining. A young refugee child came up and asked me to join in. I accepted his invitation and joined in the dancing. It was fun and exhausting but thoroughly enjoyable. A wonderful memory never to be forgotten.

Later that day I met the President of the Greek Red Cross Dr. Athanasios Doxiadis who faced the herculean task of helping the refugees in association with the assistance of the Near East Relief. As a "representative" of America, I handed over a check for three million dollars which was greatly received by Dr.Doxiadis who acknowledged the generosity of the American people. A group photo taken at the handing-over ceremony was published in Greek and American newspapers. My father was very proud to see my photo on the front pages of Trenton newspapers.

Returning to our hotel, exhaustion had overtaken me. I needed to rest and have a good night's sleep. I laid down in bed at 8 p.m. and woke up the next morning at 7.30 a.m. I wondered what would be on today's agenda. We had breakfast and were picked up from our hotel by an official Near East Relief car at 10 a.m. I asked the driver where we were going and he replied "We will be visiting the President and Prime Minister." I didn't know what to expect or what they would say to me. Anyway, I felt proud that I would be meeting the top leaders of Greece.

Arriving at the presidential palace, we were ushered into this big room and waited for the arrival of the president. His private secretary introduced the president, Pavlos Koundouriotis to our entourage who was wearing his admiral's uniform. We were told that Koundouriotis commanded the Greek navy during the Balkan Wars of 1912-13 and was responsible for sinking several Turkish cruisers. His strategy allowed the Greek navy to bottle up the remainder of the Turkish naval fleet from entering the northern Aegean Sea. A loyal officer and a close friend of former Greek premier, Eleftherios Venizelos who had served his country with honor and distinction.

Koundouriotis approached and spoke to me in English. I must say his English was good and made communication between us easy. He showed great interest in my mission to Greece and handed me a letter of thanks to give to my father. A small ceremony was conducted where he presented me with a medal for my contribution to the relief effort. Furthermore, the ceremony was filmed for posterity's sake. I was the first child to receive a medal something which I treasured for the remainder of my life. The film's message was KEEP THE BOWL FULL encouraging our fellow Americans back home to continue supporting the refugees.

With the introduction and filming out of the way, I asked the president whether he had any children. He was a softly-spoken man who told me that he had adult children. When not carrying out his political duties, he enjoyed spending time with his young grandchildren. Playing with them, and reading to them gave him great satisfaction. He was a good man who cared about his people and wanted the refugees absorbed into Greek society. Fancy me a twelve-year old conserving with President Koundouriotis something which I could brag about to my fellow students back in America. Boy, I bragged about it for some years.

Another day gone. Tomorrow we were to meet the Greek prime minister in his office at the parliamentary building. I had no idea what was on the agenda. As usual, the official Near East Relief vehicle picked us up. We arrived at 9.30 am at the prime minister's office where he greeted us in a friendly manner. He spoke to Mr.Chalmers of our Near East Relief and asked him whether I could visit an orphanage on the island of Syros. Turning to me, "Do you want to visit Syros?", Chalmers said. "Of course, I want to." Chalmers made the arrangement with the prime minister's office for our visit to Syros.

Several days later, a Greek warship took us to Syros. The journey from Piraeus to Syros took about four hours sailing with calm seas. Disembarking at Hermoupolis, my first impression was the refugee tents near the harbor. Thousands of people lived close together and their living conditions were no better than those that I had seen in Athens. We were taken on a tour of the refugee camp where I got a chance to talk with some of the children. They told me that their lives were very good in Asia Minor. They attended excellent schools, wore school uniforms, and never thought they would end up living on Syros wearing rags. These children were lucky that their parents were still alive. Unfortunately, some children had been orphaned. Their parents, grandparents, aunts, uncles, and cousins had either been massacred or deported to unknown destinations in the interior of Anatolia. No one cares for them.

Our Near East organization had created an orphanage on Syros taking in orphan children and seeking to give them a future. I visited the orphanage located in an abandoned army barracks to see first-hand how these orphans were being treated. They were provided with a bed and clean blanket to sleep on, clean clothes, three daily meals, and education, and some of the older orphans also learned carpentry and other trades. This was the American way of teaching them discipline and to become self-reliant. In other words, standing up on your own two feet and not to depend on hand-outs.

I was surprised to see how happy they were to meet me and spoke with them through an interpreter. I asked the interpreter whether the children wanted to be adopted by families. The overall answer was YES. They wanted to be part of a family where they could experience some kind of "normal life." However, a "normal life" was out of the question as many refugee parents found it difficult to take care of their own children. Some orphans hoped that rich families in Greece would adopt them or even some relatives in America. I had no idea of our nation's immigration policy and hoped some American relatives would adopt these orphans.

The orphanage organized a social event in my honor. I had no idea what it would be. The children came out of this room wearing traditional Greek costumes. They danced traditional Greek and Asia Minor dances and asked me to join in. I accepted and danced like a seasoned performer. I was a quick learner picking up the dance steps in Athens. What a great time we had dancing. It was time to head back to Piraeus.

The next morning, I embarked on my return journey to New York. I loved my Greek stay enjoying the dancing, talking to the orphan children, and meeting Greece's top political leaders. I never forgot the Greek people who thronged the streets to see me. I thought our Near East organization was doing a magnificent in caring for the refugees. Now it time had come to cross the Mediterranean and the Atlantic to see the Statute of Liberty once again. Our trip was marred by a tropical storm in the mid-Atlantic, bringing heavy seas, heavy rain, and gale-force winds. The tempest finally disappeared into the horizon. After that, it was smooth sailing all the way to New York.

Clearing customs and immigration, my father's chauffeur was waiting to take me to our family home in New Jersey. My parents and siblings ran out of the house to greet me. We embraced each other. Happiness ruled that moment. I had plenty of stories to tell the family. The next few days were spent relaxing before resuming school.

One night I told my father about the orphan children that should be allowed to come and live in America. Father was sympathetic to my idea. He suggested to our Congressman and Senator that Congress show some humanity in allowing these poor children to come to America. They liked his idea but convincing a Republican-dominated Congress and our State Department would prove difficult. It meant our government would have to make a one-off special amendment to the Immigration Act to allow the orphans to enter the United States. The orphans could only enter the US subject to having relatives who could sponsor them. Some orphans were lucky to end up living with their American relatives. Others did not have such luck.

CHAPTER 12

A MONK IN
PONTUS

A s the noose is put around my neck, death will quickly follow. I am accused of a crime that I didn't commit with the mob starring with hatred in their eyes at me. This is something unimaginable which I never contemplated four months earlier.

In June 1921, I was a monk in the Greek Orthodox monastery, St Vasilios on the outskirts of Kerasunda. We were thirty monks devoting our lives to our Lord Jesus Christ. Our daily routine was simple prayers at different times of the day, tending to our vegetable and fruit garden, and making trinkets (inexpensive toys, jewelry, and ornaments) which we sold in the marketplace in town.

One day Turkish soldiers came banging on the front entrance of the monastery shouting "Open up ! open up!". I calmly walked up to open up to them. They rushed in with fire in their eyes like wild beasts ready to devour us. One of the officers said: " I want to see your Abbott." "I will take you to him", I said. The officer introduced himself as Arif Effendi who had instructions to search the monastery for enemy documents and to ascertain if we had assisted Greek guerillas operating in our region.

Our Abbott, brother Eugenios calmly responded that our monastery wasn't involved in politics, nor did it provide any assistance to the guerillas. Arif Effendi responded that they had received information from local Turkish villagers that they had witnessed us harboring and assisting the guerillas. I knew these allegations to be untrue. Our mission as monks was to do God's work on Earth.

The soldiers searched the monastery without finding anything implicating us with the guerillas. I thought we would never see them again. A week later, they came back banging on our front entrance. I strolled up to open up wondering what they wanted this time. Opening up, the soldiers rushed in and arrested all of us. We were taken in the central prison of Kerasunda held without any formal charges against us.

During our time in jail, we were given very little food and water. They were trying to starve us to death or wear us down physically and mentally so that we would confess to assisting the guerillas. Whatever their motives, our collective consciousness was clear. We had nothing to hide and never had contact with the guerillas.

Prison conditions were horrible. We were packed like cattle with up to ten sometimes twenty prisoners in small cells. Windows were very small allowing very little fresh air to enter making us breathe stale air. We slept on cement or dirt floors with no beds or pillows. Sleeping wasn't easy especially during the July-August period as the weather was very hot. Rats, beetles, and cockroaches ran amok competing who was to be top dog in our cells. We were only allowed two hours of daily exercise where at least we could get some fresh air. The guards watched over us like hawks.

In the prison yard, we talked about our days at the monastery, our families and the sufferings of martyred saints. I felt I was persecuted for being a Christian but never compared myself to Agios Petros. The Turks always considered us infidels and treated us like second-class people. I harbored no ill-will towards them. At the monastery, we helped Turkish families or Turks who were hungry or needed assistance. Our door was open to everyone irrespective of their race or religion. I remember Jesus's parable who is my neighbor. As monks, it was our Christian duty to assist our fellow man.

I wondered when we would be released from prison since we weren't formally charged with any crime. Then came the biggest shock of all. We were hauled before the Courts of Independence accused of belonging to an organization named Pontus which wanted to establish an independent Republic along the shores of the Black Sea. Other charges were filed against us that we conspired to assist Greek marines to land in Kerasund, Samsoun, Sinope, and Trebizond to take charge of the entire region in the name of King Constantine.

We had no legal representation and had to fend for ourselves as best we could. The so-called judges, four mean individuals stared down at us like eagles ready to devour us. The 'chief judge' read out the formal charges accusing us of belonging to a conspiratorial organization named Pontus which sought to overthrow the Kemalist government and establish an independent Greek state in Pontus. I was shocked at the charges leveled against me and my fellow monks. We always minded our own business and assisted both Christians or Muslims who came to the monastery seeking assistance.

After the charges were formally readout, I declared my innocence to the 'court.' "I have never heard of the Pontus organization, I never conspired against our government in Angora and have assisted my people and brother Turks." "I am here to do God's work and am not interested in politics. I always pray for the health of our leader, Mustapha Kemal Pasha, and hope that peace can be established in our country. War has brought misery and destruction for all our people," I said.

The judges didn't believe me. They thought I was trying to cheat my way out of a jail sentence or even avoiding execution. I was taken back to my cell after giving evidence. I anxiously awaited their final decision. Meanwhile, some fellow monks were found guilty and executed for 'treason' against the Kemalist state. Somehow, my inner voice kept telling me "you will die." I tried to dismiss it but somehow felt I would suffer the same fate as them.

The next day, the judges announced their final decision. Execution would be my fate. They found me guilty of being a traitor conspiring with the enemy to destroy Kemal's army and assisting the guerillas. They threw in a new charge that I was involved in a secret group plotting the assassination of the local governor, Salim Pasha. I knew all these charges were untrue and had no avenue of appeal. The court's decision was final.

I was ready to meet my maker with a clean conscience and prayed for peace in our region.

CHAPTER 13

A TURKISH OFFICER REGRETS

I am a Turkish officer who served both in the Ottoman and Kemalist armies during the most troublesome and chaotic years of our nation's history. I shall remain anonymous to avoid my family facing reprisals from our government authorities. I witnessed many deportations, atrocities, and death which troubled my conscience since leaving the army in 1924.

During the great war, I served at Gallipoli and the Middle East and other things in-between. At Gallipoli, we defended our empire from the British and their colonial soldiers who fought heroically against us. I remember one day viewing from my binoculars, the British officers hiding in their bunker-like scared little boys whereas their colonials fought and died like heroes.

Even before the Gallipoli landing, I was ordered to remove all the Greeks from Gallipoli and banish them into Asia Minor. We showed no mercy to them. "Yiaour! Get your clothes and be ready to leave in one hour or else", I said to all of them. I made no distinction between men, women, and children in the way they were to be treated. We kept them overnight in Turkish villages before sending them into Asia Minor. As far as I know, many of them worked in the labor battalions in road construction and other works deemed necessary by the local authorities.

I had officer friends in charge of the labor battalions who told me the treatment meted out to the Greeks." We worked them hard, gave them very little or no rest working from dawn till dusk, gave them bread, water and soup until they dropped dead." During that time, I felt no sympathy for them. "No infidel in our country is a good thing", I thought to myself.

After the Gallipoli campaign, I took leave in Constantinople for a few weeks. My next assignment was in the eastern provinces of Asia Minor where the Armenians lived. I was ordered to round them up and deport them en masse into the Syrian desert. The standard phrase was "get your clothes and be ready to move." Somehow we treated the Armenians harsher than the Greeks during the Great War. As we marched into the Syrian desert, the Armenians died in great numbers from starvation, lack of water, and disease. I shot a few who tried to escape. When they complained, I whipped them so hard that they dropped to the ground pleading with me to take their lives. I had no sympathy for them. They deserved to die as they had betrayed their Sultan, country, and fellow citizens supporting the enemy.

I received instructions to command a military unit in Palestine against the British. I was lucky to escape capture and ended up in Syria. I was saddened to see Jerusalem becoming British after it had belonged to us for over 300 years. In Syria, the British succeeded in pushing us back to Damascus when we finally surrendered to them. The news came through that our empire signed the armistice at Mudros, Lemnos on October 30, 1918.

I demobilized and rejoined my family in Smyrna. My wife and children were so relieved to see me in one piece. I survived the war unscathed. I couldn't believe we lost the war and blamed our government for its close relations with Germany. The Germans weren't interested in Turkey, they simply wanted to control the riches and trade of Asia Minor through the Berlin-Baghdad railway line. Fortunately, Germany never laid its hands on our nation's natural resources. However, our enemies (Anglo-French-Italians) wanted to replace Germany as our new economic masters instead.

The Greek occupation of Smyrna had consequences far beyond anyone could have imagined in May 1919. The death of our fellow Turks in Smyrna inspired Mustapha Kemal to establish a nationalist movement to liberate our homeland from the infidel. I decided to do my patriotic duty by enlisting in Kemal's army in Angora. Leaving my family behind in Smyrna was painful but they understood my reasons for joining.

During the early stages of our conflict, the Greeks held the upper hand and enjoyed the support of their allied friends. However, the removal of Venizelos and the return of King Constantine changed the situation in our favor. The allies abandoned the yiaour and opened up dialogue with Kemal. Of course, the turning point in the war was the Greek's failure to defeat us outside Angora.

In early 1922, I was sent to fight Greek guerrillas in Pontus. They put up fierce resistance but we defeated them and took control of the region. As part of our military mission, we inspected Greek villages to see if they were hiding weapons and guerrillas. In some villages, we arrested villagers who assisted the guerrillas by deporting them into the Anatolian interior. They suffered the same fate as their fellow Greeks and Armenians during the great war. History repeated itself as I commanded a unit in the deportations from Pontus. Death was the best that could happen to these betrayers.

At last, our homeland was free. Kemal's brilliant army ousted the infidel from Turkish soil. I remember when I entered Smyrna with my unit feeling proud seeing our people smile. The tears of the last three years were permanently wiped away. Then a great fire engulfed Smyrna. I believe the Greeks and Armenians were responsible for lighting it and blaming us for it. The Smyrna quay was full of yiaours who sought escape from the ravaging inferno calling out to the British, French, Italians, and Americans to save them. I didn't care whether they survived or died. I didn't want these back-stabbers remaining in Turkey.

After the fire, we arrested and deported Ottoman Greek males aged 17-45 into the interior to work in the labor battalions. Some of them had collaborated with the Greeks. I know very few of them survived their ordeal. I was honorably discharged from the army and returned to my family in 1924.

Upon leaving the army, I had a dream that Allah visited me one night and said " what did you do to these poor innocent people. They never harmed you. How will you atone for your sins?." Suddenly I woke up with my conscience pricked with memories of these dead people. I prayed to Allah begging forgiveness for my sins. I told my family about my encounter with Allah and regretted my past deeds. My children were taught "never hate, do good and help people."

CHAPTER 14

SMYRNA: THE LAST GREEK CITY IN ASIA MINOR

My New York newspaper, the Tribune Herald sent me in 1908 to be their correspondent in Constantinople to cover events in the Near East. I was stationed in the beautiful capital of the Ottoman Empire, Constantinople with its magnificent landmarks of the Aghia Sophia, Topkapi Palace, the Seraglio, Christian churches, Mosques, and bazaars. I established close contact with certain Ottoman Ministers who gave me confidential information of political events unfolding in the Empire. I never revealed their identities in my reports sent to our New York office.

I covered the Young Turk revolution of 1908, the Balkan and First World Wars, and the Greek landing in Smyrna on May 15, 1919. I fell in love with Smyrna with its great night life, business activity, theatre productions, opera nights, dancing and singing outside the Greek restaurants. I heard many foreign languages and marvelled its famous educational institutions which possessed great libraries.

My editor sent me urgently to report on the last days of the Greek administration of Smyrna in early September 1922. Though I didn't personally witness the great fire of Smyrna, I could see the flames engulfing the city on board our US warship: Abraham Lincoln. I was very emotional seeing the quay thronged with thousands of refugees seeking to escape the brutalities of the Turks. Our warships and so-called allied friends did not lift a finger to save these poor wretched souls.

After witnessing such a great human catastrophe, my editor telegraphed me to return to New York. My 15 exciting years as a correspondent for my newspaper had come to an end in the Near East. The editor told me that many of our readers were interested in learning more about Smyrna. I was engaged for the three months collecting information to write a piece on Smyrna. Meanwhile, I covered the politics of New York. Finally, my Smyrna piece appeared in our supplement: Current Events which was well received by our readership. Many readers wrote letters to the editor appreciating my piece.

My article is reproduced in full below:

Smyrna was a vibrant and exciting city prior to its occupation and destruction by Turkish forces on September 13, 1922. After defeating the Greek army, Mustapha Kemal's forces entered Smyrna on September 9 thus ending three millennia of Hellenic civilization in Asia Minor. The Great Idea (Megali Idea) which dominated Greek foreign policy from the inception of the fledgling Greek Kingdom in the 1830's was now in tatters. Smyrna was a major commercial port which also enjoyed a rich social, cultural and sporting life.

Before 1922, Smyrna was a cosmopolitan city with a population of 270,000 inhabitants composed of 140,000 Greeks, 80,000 Turks, 12,000 Armenians, 20,000 Jews and 15,000 Europeans including Levantines. The latter were descendants of British, Italian, Dutch, and French who had settled earlier in the Near East. They resided outside of Smyrna in the two small towns of Boudja and Bournabat. Smyrna was divided into Greek, Turkish, Armenian and Jewish quarters showing the ethnic and social divide of the city.

The Smyrna- Aidin railway owned by British interests was important in the export trade of Smyrna. This railway assisted in moving the agricultural produce of Smyrna's hinterland and Central Anatolia to foreign markets. Greek peasant farmers produced figs, currants, olives and tobacco crops. The Greek middle and educated classes were composed of clerks, shopkeepers, salaried men doctors, lawyers and teachers. Rich Greek merchants lived in exclusive suburbs of Smyrna. A survey conducted by Smyrna economist, John B.Yannikis revealed that there were 391 factories in 'greater Smyrna' of which 344 belonged to Greeks who employed 4584 workers and 485 clerical staff.

There were large American interests at Smyrna including Standard Oil Company, MacAndrews and Forbes licorice firm, major tobacco firms, and carpet manufacturers. The British and French bought the agricultural produce from Smyrna's hinterland. Some of the British firms were C.Whittall &Co, Anglo-Anatolian Trading Co, and Anglo-Oriental Trading Co. There also existed four Chambers of Commerce: Greek, French, British and Italian.

Smyrna had a rich social life where Smyrniotes enjoyed dances, musical afternoons and evenings given in the wealthy salons of the affluent Greeks and Armenians. Greek and Armenian women wore the latest fashions from Paris and London. There were four large clubs: the Cercle de Smyrne patronized mostly by British, French, and Americans, along with the Sporting, the Greek and Country clubs with the different ethnic groups socializing and establishing contacts.

The establishment of schools, theaters, literary societies, sporting clubs and newspapers played an important role in the maintenance of the Greek language, identity, national consciousness and cultural heritage in Smyrna. There were many Greek schools with the most notable ones being the Central School of St.Photini (1833) and the Homerian (1881) both for young girls and the Greco-German and Greco-French lyceums. The Evangelical School (1733) was the most famous well endowed and possessing an excellent library.

Aristidis Sterghiadis, the Greek High Commissioner May 1919-September 1922, was responsible along with Professor Constantine Karatheodoris in establishing a university in Smyrna which never operated due to the occupation of the city by the Kemalists .

International college of Smyrna (1891) established by Reverend Dr. Alexander MacLachan was formally recognized by Turkish authorities where it accepted Greek, Armenian, and Turkish students. It closed down by shifting its operations to Beirut, Lebanon in 1934.

The theater was alive and well in Smyrna. The following theaters: Efterpi (1841), Kamerano (1862), Alhambra and Eldorado being open air, Sporting Club (1894), Havouza (1900), Gay (1909), the Splendid and Kremer were established to cater for performances by major European and Greek theatrical groups. It should be noted that smaller theaters operated in the neighborhoods and suburbs of Smyrna. Professional Smyrna theater companies such as Arts Players, Patriotic Players, and Smyrna Musical Players used their art to express the political aspects of the Greek-Turkish conflict. The last performance ended with the closure of Greek theaters in the summer of 1922.

It also had its own literary societies such as the Omonoia Reading Society (1865), Smyrna Drama Society (1870), Shakespeare Drama Society (1905) and Arts Society of Smyrna (1919) which indicated a well-educated population who appreciated literature for its own sake. Daily Greek, French, Armenian, Jewish and Turkish newspapers kept their respective communities informed of local and international events. Greek dailies included: Amaltheia, Kosmos, Omonoia, Patris, Telegraphos, Tharros, Estia and Vima. Some of the newspaper owners and journalists received their education at the Evangelical School which was only American school in Smyrna.

Greek publishing houses produced scientific and satirical journals. Some of the important ones were Eranastis, Aristotelis, and Nea Zoe. The first one focused on scientific, historical and philosophical whereas the second concentrated on religious and encyclopedic articles. Nea Zoe published poems and also gave Elias Venezis, the author of the book The number 31328 , an outlet for his first stories and series of sonnets. It also raised the issue of women's rights which would have a controversial issue in a male-dominated society. Satirical publications like Techni, Smyrnaios (1920), Peirasmos (May 1922) and Kopanos (1908) would have kept Smyrniotes amused. Techni printed philological and sociological articles and also provided a translation of foreign literary works and book reviews.

Sporting clubs had 'its roots in the city's music and intellectual societies.' The Orpheus Club (1890) organized gymnastics, athletics, artistic and literary events whereas the Apollon Club (1891) arranged boat races, boxing, and football. Apollon played football matches against local teams and foreign crews of ships visiting the port. The merger of Orpheus and Gymnasion resulted in the formation of the Panionios Sporting Club in 1898 who offered gymnastics, athletics, and football. It participated in all Panionian games until 1922 and some of its athletes participated in the 1906, 1912 and 1920 Olympic Games for Greece. As part of its charter, membership was open to anyone including women. Other clubs included Sporting (1896) and Pelops (1908) who held the last swimming races in July 1922.

On the medical front, St Haralambos was the major Greek hospital had wards "for surgery, pathology,gynecology, ophthalmology, mental maladies,...maternity department [and] old peoples' asylum." It treated all comers without distinction of nationality or religion. During the

Great War, the Ottoman authorities took charge of this hospital with a reduction in medical services. Those who couldn't afford to pay were treated free of charge. It resumed normal operation in 1919.

Smyrna was an exciting place to live with its multiethnic populace and babel of languages which gave its cosmopolitan nature. The jewel of the Near East, also known as Gavur Izmir (infidel Smyrna) ended in ashes by the Turks in September 1922.

CHAPTER 15

THREE GREEK-AMERICANS IN ASIA MINOR

My name is Kostas (Gus) Paskavoglou, and I am originally from Smyrna in Asia Minor. I came to America with my two brothers: Andreas (Andy) and Mihalis (Mike) just before the outbreak of the Balkan Wars in October 1912. I chose to Anglicize my family name to Paskas to make it easier for Americans to pronounce it. They had difficulties saying foreign names. My brothers kept our family name.

We cleared immigration on Ellis island and stayed a couple of nights with friends in New York. We caught the train for Boston and were picked up by family friends from the train station who took us to Lowell. Lowell is a manufacturing town with many Greeks and other nationalities working as factory laborers. The working day was long for low pay. At least we were able to earn an income.

We were lucky to speak several languages, including English, which learned in Smyrna. It was easy for us to communicate with Americans, French, Italians, Turks, and Germans. You heard this babble of languages in Lowell.

We rented a cheap apartment not far from our work and paid two dollars per week in rent. We pooled our money to ensure that we could meet our daily expenses in our new homeland. We managed to save a little money for a rainy day. We also wired money to help our parents in Smyrna. They were not wealthy at all but depended on our wealth to make ends meet.

After several years, our financial position improved and didn't like the idea of working in a factory. We decided to start up our own business. We explored several ideas before deciding on the type of company we wanted to create. Though we liked Lowell and had made lots of friends, we needed to advance our interests.

I came up with the idea of opening up a candy store either in Chicago or New York, which had many of our compatriots living in these two cities. We agreed to move to New York in June 1916. America still hadn't entered the war.

We found a vacant building in Astoria, where we established our candy store selling candy, ice cream, lemonade, and flowers. At the start, the business was slow but gradually improved as our customers got to know us because of our low prices and friendly service.

We became American citizens at the end of the World War and were glad we came to live in this great land. America was our refuge away from the troubles of the Ottoman Empire. I remember reading about the Armenian massacres and later about our compatriots in the Black Sea region.

We never forgot our beautiful Smyrna and our parents, whom we hadn't seen in many years. In May 1919, we read in the local Greek and American press of the Greek troop landing in Smyrna. We were excited to see our beloved city coming under Greek control. The Turks hated it, but we didn't care too much about their opinion.

In early 1921, my two brothers and I visited the Greek Consulate in New York to enlist as volunteers in the Greek army. The Consular (Mr.Panopoulos) was surprised at our decision since we're American citizens. I told him that " we are very proud of our Greek heritage and wish to ensure that Smyrna stays Greek, not Turkish." We read in the National Herald and Atlantis of our military successes in Asia Minor, where such stories inspired us to do our patriotic duty.

We left New York in late April bound for Athens and eventually onto Smyrna. Meanwhile, we left our most trusted employee, Nick Psaros, to run the business during our absence. We prepared a legal document with our lawyer to transfer the ownership of our business to Nick just in case something untoward happened to us.

We finally arrived in Smyrna in late June after doing some of our military training just outside Athens. Within a couple of weeks, we saw combat action on the Asia Minor front. My unit participated in the capture of Afion Karahissar, whereas my brothers were at Eskishehr.

We were excited at the prospect of occupying the Kemalist capital, Angora (Ankara). We marched through flat terrain devoid of trees before reaching a high plateau with our Angora in our sight. We camped some 30 miles outside Angora, ready for our assault. The next day, our commander belted out instructions of what positions we were taking and hold. Yes! We were ready to go.

The Turks attacked on a broad front, pushing us back, but we counter-attacked, pushing our enemy to the outskirts of their capital. I thought that Angora would fall to us, and the Turks would surrender. They didn't and fought tenaciously to defend their capital.

The Turks counter-attacked and pushed us back beyond the Sangarios River. A golden opportunity was lost, and we ended up holding the Afion Karahissar-Eskishehr defensive line. We lost many excellent soldiers, and some of them became prisoners of war. I don't know what our actual casualty figures were and what happened to our prisoners of war.

It was frustrating holding such an expanded defensive position where the Turks could easily attack us with impunity. Our troop morale reached rock bottom with many of our comrades who didn't have leave for some time. They were tired, bored, and angry, wanting to see their families. For us, America was our home. It was too far to return to New York.

In late August 1922, the Turks surprised us by attacking on a broad front. We retreated towards the coast demoralized, dispirited, and bewildered towards Smyrna. Thousands of refugees fled with us, seeking their escape from the firestorm that would be unleashed by the Kemalists.

I was lucky to be evacuated along with other soldiers to the Greek mainland. As we departed Smyrna, there were thousands of refugees thronged along the quay seeking their salvation. We couldn't help them, which included our parents.

I arrived in Piraeus and considered myself lucky to have survived my ordeal. I made inquiries with the Greek military authorities to find out the fate of my two brothers. I was told they had been taken as prisoners of war. I will continue this story at a future date.

CHAPTER 16

A FRENCH CONSUL IN SMYRNA

I am Jacques Moreaux who served as the French Consul-General in Smyrna before and after the Great War. My role was to protect and advance French interests in a volatile region of the Ottoman Empire.

Before 1914, I remember the Ottoman Turks engaged in conflict with their neighbors during the Balkan Wars. It was a brutal bloody war with many casualties on all sides. When conflict broke out in October 1912, the Ottoman authorities ordered every Turk aged 18-45 to register in the army to fight the infidel. The recruiting stations were overflowing with enthusiastic young men ready to do their patriotic for the Sultan and Empire. The local Greeks, Bulgarians, and Serbians kept a low profile to avoid Turkish reprisals.

Our consulate was located not too far from the Greek quarter of Smyrna. As I walked about the Greek neighborhood, I saw Ottoman flags displayed outside Greek shops as a mark of loyalty towards the Empire. I wondered whether this loyalty was sincere or simply a front. It probably was a protective measure by the owners to protect their businesses from looting and protecting their families out of harm's way. These businesses were left unscathed during the conflict. Generally, the Greeks kept a low profile thus avoiding the attention of the Turkish authorities.

After the signing of the Treaty of Bucharest and Athens Convention in August and November 1913, the attitude of the Turks changed towards the Greeks. Many Muslims in Macedonia and Thrace abandoned their homes and properties and sought refuge on Turkish soil. The Ottoman government moved them into Christian villages outside of Smyrna which inflamed the situation between Greeks and Turks. This was a deliberate policy measure to force the Greeks to leave their villages and seek refuge in Greece or the nearby islands.

The Turks boycotted Greek businesses, attacked Greeks in the streets, and the Turkish press ran articles inflaming an already explosive situation. Press articles encouraged violence and hatred towards Greeks on a scale that I never experienced as a diplomat. The local Greek newspapers encouraged their compatriots to reach out to their Turkish neighbors that both were born and shared the same homeland. This enmity wasn't good for peace in Smyrna or the Ottoman fatherland (Vatan).

The Greek premier, Venizelos, and the Grand Vizier worked towards a voluntary exchange of populations which I thought was a good solution in defusing a potential conflict between Greece and Turkey. As talks were underway hammering details of the exchange of population and compensation for abandoned properties, the Ottoman government declared war against my country and our allies in late October 1914.

I immediately asked for my diplomatic passport and left Smyrna on board a warship for Marseilles. From there I proceeded to Paris to report to our Foreign Ministry on the situation in Smyrna. In my report, I mentioned that our investments in railways and trade would be severely affected by the war. I also negotiated with the

Turkish Governor to allow our citizens some of who were Greek to leave unmolested. He honored his agreement and gave us 24 hours to leave Smyrna. Our citizens left their deposits in the branches of the Credit Lyonnais and the Imperial Ottoman Bank who came to France practically penniless. The issues of investments and bank deposits would be taken up during the peace conference.

I was assigned to the Near East desk in the Foreign Ministry to analyze military intelligence reports and work closely with our allies in Paris. However, I was unhappy with my role and wanted to do my patriotic duty. So, I joined the army and served as an officer on the western front. The Germans got very close to overrunning Paris but our army fought like the possessed driving the enemy almost to the Belgian border. Our beautiful Paris was spared the Hun occupation. Echoes of 1871 were still remembered in 1917.

Finally, November 11, 1918, had arrived, armistice day, the Germans surrendered and off to the peace table in 1919. I was off to Smyrna to resume my consular duties in April 1919. It was wonderful to return to this beautiful cosmopolitan city with its rich cultural and educational life. We had a few French schools operating in Smyrna. Some of our French citizens started returning to Smyrna to resume their lives.

In May, I was thrilled to see the Greek warships enter Smyrna harbor with their troops ready to take control of the city on behalf of the allies. The local Greeks were ecstatic to see their compatriots marching from the quay to Government House to hoist the Greek flag. Then the unexpected happened. Shots were fired from unknown assailants making the Greeks return the fire.

What ensued was murder, looting, and destruction of Turkish lives and properties by the local Greeks. This wasn't the start the Greek administration wanted. The Greeks needed to do something to improve their image in Smyrna. Premier Venizelos sent his close friend Aristidis Sterghiadis to be High Commissioner to undertake this difficult mission. Upon arrival, Sterghiadis let it be known that he had come to establish law and order and any violations of the law wouldn't be tolerated.

He was a man of his word. Those responsible for the recent events were arrested and found guilty were either executed or sent to long prison sentences. The local Greeks hated him and accused him of being pro-Turk and acting like a dictator. He issued a press release stating that his role was to be impartial and protect both Christian and Muslims. Many Turks respected him for his impartiality and fairness. I got on very well with him. We had many long conversations regarding Greco-French relations. Sterghiadis spoke French fluently with an excellent French accent.

The Greek administration proved effective under Sterghiadis even with the change of government in Athens in November 1920. The Royalists respected and asked him to continue at his post. I detested Royalist government but this never changed my good relations and friendship with Aristidis. He loyally served his country with honor and distinction.

Then came September 1922 with the Greeks ejected from Asia Minor. Our government dispatched warships to safely evacuate our nationals from Smyrna. One of my last consular duties was giving the Ottoman Greeks certificates of French citizenship to leave for France. I wasn't supposed to do this but my sense of humanity got the better of me. I boarded the Edgar Quinet leaving this magnificent city with a raging inferno in the background for Piraeus and finally Paris.

I will never forget Smyrna.

CHAPTER 17

FROM CAPPADOCIA TO SALONIKA

I am recounting the story my parents told me growing up in Greece. My family came from the small town of Sinasos situated in central Cappadocia where many Karamanlides and Turks lived peacefully together for many centuries. Our neighbors were kind gentlefolk who invited us to their family weddings and other family celebrations. I was five years including my two siblings when my parents and we were forcibly exchanged from Sinasos to go to live in Greece in 1923.

In Sinasos, my father, George Koramoglou owned a small store producing and selling all different types of jewelry. His jewelry was regarded as of high quality by his customers and continued the same tradition later in Greece. Our family was well-known and well respected by everyone in the town. I never heard my father utter a bad word about the townsfolk. He said it was the war between the Greeks and Turks that brought this catastrophe upon us. George had no idea where Constantinople or Greece was located on a map. Sinasos and the surrounding area were our universe.

Sometimes our parents and neighbors would go together on picnics not far from our town to enjoy a beautiful sunny summer day. As children we played our childhood games like hide and seek and who was the fastest to climb a tree. I climbed it like a monkey. Winters were very cold and bitter with lots of snow as well. We always managed to keep our house warm. I remember playing with our neighbors' kids in the snow. We had many snow fights. It was fun.

Our town had two schools- one for the Karamanlides and Turks. The children of the Karamanlides wrote Turkish using Greek letters whereas the Turks' children were schooled in the Ottoman script so George said. Even our Orthodox Church services were conducted in Turkish. I have no recollection of this but accept what George said.

George said the years, 1912-1922 were one of conflict, hatred, and massacre. He heard that the Young Turks in Constantinople had ordered the deportation and massacre of countless Armenians and later the Greeks. He remembered seeing convoys of Armenian men, women, and children deportees being marched off into oblivion. He figured out the meaning of the word-oblivion. The Greeks experienced the same fate as their Armenian counterparts. For unknown reasons, we Karamanlides escaped deportation. Maybe because we're Turkish-speaking rather than Greek and Armenian. Our Turkish neighbors never threatened us during this momentous time. Relations between us were cordial and friendly. At least, my family survived this terrible ordeal.

The Greek army wasn't far from our town as it pursued the Kemalists to Ankara. George later learned in Greece that there was fierce fighting from the combatants with each seeking to deliver the fatal blow. Neither side was able to deliver the knock-out punch so a stalemate ensued. I recall George saying it was nearly 12 months. Then, the Kemalists delivered their killer blow in August 1922 by driving the Greeks out of Asia Minor. There was great jubilation throughout Turkey over Mustapha Kemal's victory. Our family shared in the celebrations.

What followed for us was incomprehensible to my family. The new regime drove the Sultan out of Constantinople and established themselves as the official government of Turkey. Karamanlides like Greeks and Armenians became undesirables in our own homeland. We had no place here, we're no longer considered citizens of this new Turkey. We had to leave, and go where? A question that greatly bothered my parents.

Kemalist officials came to Sinasos to conduct a census so we're told. The reality was the opposite. They came to find out who were Christians and Muslim residents. They separated us into two groups and we're were marched off to an internment camp not far from Sinasos. Conditions were atrocious; people were packed like sardines; slept outside in the bitter cold; some died from exposure whilst others survived; we're given little food to eat; the Kemalists tried to starve to death. We were taken to a nearby lake accompanied by Turkish guards to bathe and even drink the brackish water. Our spirits may have been "low" but the will to survive triumphed in the end.

Finally, the order had come for us to leave. We marched from near Sinasos to somewhere near the Turkish coast. George couldn't remember the town or village there. He remembers a Greek ship taking us to Greece. Along the way, we stopped at some Greek islands full of refugees dazed and traumatized losing everything they once possessed and enjoyed in Asia Minor. Our family shared the same shock and emotion as these refugees.

We arrived in Piraeus, I think, it was September 1923 with very possessions. At least, we stayed together as a family. From Athens, we're relocated to a refugee camp outside Salonika. Our major obstacle, we couldn't speak Greek. We're Turkish-speaking Karamanlides. "We're called Turko-sporoi (Turkish seed) and go back to Turkey by the local Greeks ", George recalled. Turkish seed is a derogatory term meaning we're unwanted and viewed as second-class citizens. I experienced the same racism and epithets at school. As we learned to read and write in Greek, the locals began to accept us as "Greeks." They were some who didn't want us in Greece.

George worked in a carpet factory in Salonika saving his money to open up a jewelry store. We lived in a neighborhood composed of Asia Minor refugees. We all shared the same memories of Asia Minor-self-reliance, living a comfortable life, and having a good education. Maybe this is why the local Greeks despised us and were jealous of us. George opened up his store and continued producing high-quality jewelry which received praise from his clientele.

Greece was our home, we could never return to Sinasos. I remember George saying this before his death in 1940.

Ismet Pasha and Venizelos came.

And they decided they would a trade

I wonder if they thought to ask a soul.

We left our churches, and our schools behind

We lost our money, lost our property

We cursed the authors of the antallayi (exchange)

Each one of us was cast away to sea.

CHAPTER 18

A GRANDFATHER'S TALL TALE

My grandchildren asked me to recount my experiences having fought at Gallipoli, Middle East, and the Greek-Turkish War. As the First World War began, I lived in New York as a Greek immigrant who wished to fight for the old country. I went to the British Consulate by offering my services as a volunteer. They accepted me after passing the medical. I wanted to fight the Turks. These encounters brought back memories that I buried deep into my subconscious.

I remember my Gallipoli experience in 1915. I explained that war was brutal, harsh, and cruel. You see fellow soldiers were maimed, injured, or killed in front of my very eyes. I didn't know whether I would live to fight and see another day. I consider myself fortunate in surviving the horrors of the Great War.

At Gallipoli, we fought Turks who defended their homeland from us. They viewed us as the enemy seeking to occupy their capital, Constantinople. How I survived unscathed at Gallipoli, God only knows. I consider myself lucky. Some invisible hands protected me so I could live to tell my story to you. Remember, war isn't fun, it's serious business where people die.

Shells exploded in front and behind me, I was scared out of my wits but my instincts of survival were stronger than my fear of death. I simply wanted to live. Life was too precious to lose. Yes! I survived.

During the night, we rested in our trenches talking about the day's battle of how it unfolded and remembering about our families back home. Thinking about our families kept us going that we would see them at the end of hostilities. Writing letters to mom and dad was another way of keeping in touch with them. Some comrades never returned. They were killed by exploding shells, a thrown hand grenade, or rifle fire. I saw fellow soldiers bayonetted by the enemy. We couldn't help them as the shell fire was intense. Our medical personnel couldn't retrieve them to give them medical care. They were left to die alone on the battlefield. When the action quietened down, our stretcher bearers would rush out to retrieve the injured risking their personal lives. The injured received medical attention for their wounds whilst others were operated on by surgeons.

Gallipoli was one large graveyard full of dead bodies. The white flag was hoisted giving both sides the chance to bury their dead. The numerous flies and stench from decaying bodies were unbearable. We couldn't stand the smell. After that, shooting and mayhem resumed without due consideration. The Turks were pleased when we evacuated Gallipoli Peninsula saving their empire from foreign occupation. Of course, after World War 1 that would be a different story.

My unit was transferred to fight in the Middle East. We rested in Cairo, Egypt for about a month before heading off to the Sinai Peninsula to fight the Turks. During my short stay in Cairo, I became friends with some people of the Greek community there. They were hospitable and asked me how as a Greek-American I decided to join the British army when the US was neutral. I told them that I wanted to play my part in defeating the Turks.

Fighting alongside Australian, Indian, Canadian, and British troops in the Sinai campaign was to prove the beginning of the end for the Ottomans in the Middle East. I remember the Australians inflicting heavy losses on the Turks with their impressive

cavalry charges. The weather was very hot and some days proved unbearable. We were lucky we had enough water for our daily needs. Otherwise, you died of thirst in the hot desert. Finally, we pushed the Turks back to the outskirts of Jerusalem. They surrendered to the British General, Allenby granting us the opportunity to march as liberators into the holy city. A historical moment of my life being a part of the occupying force ending Ottoman rule in Palestine. I visited our Greek Orthodox Church in Jerusalem lit a candle for the city to return to Christianity.

In September-October 1918, I fought in Syria which led to the capitulation of the Ottomans. We occupied Damascus where the inhabitants were jubilant to see the allied occupying force. I met some local Greeks who were pleased to have met a Greek-American who was a member of the British army. At last, the Ottomans surrendered at Lemnos on October 30 thus ending their involvement in the Great War. The allied battle began to see what would happen to the Ottoman Empire. Would it survive or be torn to shreds?

In early December, I took my leave in Constantinople and remained there until May 1919. What a magnificent city with its fine churches, mosques, mansions, and huge marketplaces. Every language spoken on earth could be heard in the Sultan's capital. Constantinople was under allied occupation and control. Even Greece had a presence here as well. I was rapped to see Greek troops a part of the allied occupying force. The Turks may have been put up with the British and others but not the Greeks. They viewed us as infidels.

I left the British and joined the Greek army which was ready to go to Smyrna. When we landed there, I felt like someone ready to encounter another important historical episode in my life. It was sensational seeing our fellow Greeks throwing their hats in the air, the women seeing songs of freedom, and the children dressed in their best clothes. A nasty incident happened with shots being fired which resulted in the death of many Turks. Turkish businesses and properties were looted and destroyed by our local Greek Smyrniotes. That wasn't a good start for us.

The Greek Premier appointed his friend Aristidis Sterghiades as High Commissioner to administer Smyrna on behalf of the allies. Sterghiadis ordered the arrest of the individuals responsible for the deaths of the Turks and the destruction to Turkish property. These individuals were tried with some Smyrniot Greeks being hanged and other receiving harsh prison sentences. No doubt Sterghiades was unpopular and reviled by the Smyrniotes. They believed rightly or wrongly that he favoured the Turks over the Greeks.

My unit ventured outside the city repelling the Turks at Menemen, Ushak, and many other towns along the Smyrna-Kassaba railway line. The Turks fought bravely to stop us but we were far better organized and disciplined force than them. We were there to stay. These victories quickly filtered back to Smyrna with our Smyriotes overjoyed hearing about our successes.

I was involved in our attack on Ankara in 1921. It was a bloody fierce encounter with two evenly matched armies. We did our best to defeat the Turks but couldn't deliver the killer punch. So we retreated onto our defensive line when I asked to take leave in Smyrna. I got injured and asked to be relieved permanently from duty. After a medical examination, my request was accepted, and returned to the US.

I had some problems trying to re-enter the US but after telling my story to immigration officials. They finally let me back in. My grandkids thought it was a great story. I thought so too. I added a bit of salt and pepper to make it interesting for them.

CHAPTER 19

THE BAGLAMA ARTIST

I remember my wonderful days in Smyrna which Turks renamed Izmir. I was born in the village of Asnalapa outside Koutaya in 1899 to a humble Greek family who lived there for many generations. It was a mixed village where Greeks, Armenians, and Turks intermingled. Everyone knew one another. These are never-to-be-forgotten moments that shouldn't be forgotten when neighbors helped and visited each other.

All this changed with the defeat of the Greek army in September 1922. Hatred, ------ redundant, religious intolerance, murder, pillaging, and plundering became the order of the day. The Turks were hellbent on expelling all us infidels from the new Turkey. So we became refugees and set off to a new homeland that we never knew or knew us. Many Greeks didn't like us at the start, but, over time, they got used to our presence.

From a young age, I loved music and my father was an accomplished baglama performer. Everyone in the village invited him to play at weddings, christenings, and special occasions. Even the Turks loved him for his baglama. My father had a small orchestra that included Armenians and Turks, who were like a close-knit family. I remember at one Greek wedding, the bridegroom paid my father extra money to play into the early hours of the next morning, so enjoyable was his playing.

I always accompanied my father wherever he played and watched him closely how his fingers ran smoothly over the bridge of the baglama. The baglama was an extension of his personality. I wanted to learn how to play like him.   THERE were no music teachers in our village. Only my father could teach me how to play it. In-between his work and performances, he made time to teach me. I was a quick learner. Eventually, I became a member of his orchestra. I wanted to become a professional musician. Musical opportunities were very limited in Asnalapa.

I hopped on the train bound for Smyrna in 1919. I heard there were many opportunities to earn a good living as a musician there. When I arrived, I had no idea where I would be staying or finding work. It was like taking a trip into the unknown. I walked from the train station to the Greek quarter of the city. There I saw an advert in a restaurant window wanting a full-time baglamarist. I went inside and told the manager (George Avlandis) that I needed the work. "Can you play a couple of tunes for me?", he said.

I played my baglama like a true professional, with my fingers running like clockwork over the bridge and started singing as well. He was so impressed with my performance he said, " You're hired. Can you start tonight?."

"Of course. What time do you want me to come back?" I asked.

"Come back at 8 PM, as we stay open until 2 AM", George said. Before leaving, I asked George where I could find suitable accommodation. He announced that he had a spare room at his house, which he offer me at a modest rent including meals. I accepted.

I came back just before 8 PM and George introduced me to my new fellow musicians. We played like a well-oiled machine and the patrons were enthusiastic with my playing and singing. It was a good start to my musical career in Smyrna. Night after night, we played with such passion that the patrons left feeling that they had touched heaven. My colleagues and I had become very good friends over the next couple of years.

Then August-September 1922 came like a typhoon, sweeping all the Greeks away from the western shores of Asia Minor. Some of us remained behind, ending up being conscripted into the infamous labor battalions to work in road construction and bridge repairs. We're to be taken to Ankara. We marched past many Turkish villages where the Turks threw stones, spat at us, called us infidels, and even brandished knives and swords, threatening to cut us into small pieces.

Along our journey to Ankara, we slept in open fields with little food or water. The days were hot, but the nights were frigid. We're heavily guarded. Anyone attempting to escape was shot immediately and their corpse was left to the wild animals and birds to devour. I simply wanted to survive. Those of us who survived our ordeal were entertained at night by my baglama. Our spirits were raised momentarily, forgetting our suffering. Even the Turkish sentries enjoyed our performance. I was surprised that they even let us play. Singing Turkish songs was the key to our survival.

After ten days, we arrived at Asnalapa. Suddenly, I was gripped with the nostalgia of a time when Greeks, Turks, and Armenians lived side-by-side as neighbors and as friends. My family was no longer here. I had no idea of what happened to them. The Turks accommodated us in a large warehouse with little ventilation and no sunlight.

One morning, the sentries came and took ten of us Greeks and executed them in an open field behind the warehouse. The rifle shots could be heard, sending shivers up my spine. Fear gripped my whole body, I froze like an iceberg. I thought I would suffer the same fate.

During that night, I prayed incessantly to my patron saint seeking his intercession so my soul might be spared by the almighty.

The next morning, along with nine others, we were being marched off to meet our creator. Out of nowhere, a Turkish villager (Ali) appeared and shouted at the sentry. "Stop. I know Ioannis Gavralas. Our families were good friends. He plays the baglama," he uttered. Ali's intervention saved our lives. I believe God must have found my prayers acceptable and had further plans for my life.

Finally, we arrived in Ankara not knowing where we would end up. They took us to an army barracks surrounded by a barbed wire outside the city. The sentries were humorless, cruel, and showed no emotion. They hit us with their rifle butts and kicked us around like a ball. Black bruises were etched like a map on my body.

Good news. An international commission arrived in Akara, as part of the exchange of population between Greece and Turkey in 1924. We left Smyrna and arrived at our home in Athens. I continued to play the baglama for many years old age caught up with me. I am now on a government pension.

The baglama saved my life.

CHAPTER 20

AN AMERICAN DIPLOMAT IN CONSTANTINOPLE

I am an American diplomat who served his nation loyally in London, Paris, and Berlin over the last twenty years each with each post having its own unique set of problems and successes. My last post was about Constantinople which proved to be the most exciting and eventful of them all.

I arrived in June 1908 to replace my good friend Frank Schwartz who was about to retire from the diplomatic corps. Just below the surface was bubbling an earthquake that would rock Constantinople and the Ottoman Empire to its core. It was an event that would have a wide-reaching impact throughout every city and village of the Empire.

A group of young Turkish officers staged a coup in Salonika demanding the reintroduction of the 1876 Constitution, calling for parliamentary elections, and the Sultan abandoning his autocratic rule. This became known as the Young Turk revolution which quickly spread to Constantinople and cities in Asia Minor. These young officers led by Enver, Talaat, and Djavid came to Constantinople demanding Sultan Abdul Hamid 11 would be dethroned if he continued with his authoritarian rule. He had no choice but to comply with their dictates.

I was only here a month with the streets of Constantinople thronged with its citizens embracing each other like never before. Christians and Muslims calling each other brothers and sisters and all supporting the young Turks. These remarkable scenes were overflowing with joy, camaraderie, and happiness which didn't last very long. The Sultan staged a counter-coup in 1909 which the Young Turk regime brutally put down. His Majesty was imprisoned in Topkapi palace until he died in 1918.

Our government remained neutral throughout the Young Turk revolution. I was pleased to see the reopening of parliament, the staging of elections, and citizens' civil rights were protected and guaranteed under the 1876 Constitution. The Christians of the Empire were pleased to have a voice through their representatives in the Ottoman Chamber. For a short time, there was a sense of trust by the Christians until the Young Turks changed direction. The Armenian massacres in Adana in 1909 shook the faith of the Greeks and Armenians in Constantinople in the Young Turk regime. Liberty, Fraternity, and Brotherhood of 1908 seemed like an empty slogan.

War clouds were becoming darker and darker in 1911 with the Ottoman Empire finally going to war against Italy in Tripoli and Cyrenaica. The situation was tense for Italians domiciled in Constantinople who kept a low profile throughout the entire conflict. When peace was finally signed in October 1912, Italians started coming out of their shells. It was wonderful to see Italians and Turks interacting with each other once again.

The poor Ottoman Empire finished one conflict and entered another one with the Balkan League (Greece, Bulgaria, Serbia, and Montenegro) in October 1912. I saw many young Arabs, Turks, and Kurds rushing to enlist in the Ottoman army to fight the League. There were Constantinopolitan Greeks and Armenians who showed their loyalty in joining the Ottoman army during this brutal conflict. At one point in the war, the Bulgarian army was knocking at the door of Constantinople but cholera and dysentery took a death heavy toll on them allowing the Turks to defend their city.

The combatants signed a series of treaties and conventions establishing peace, settling frontiers, and allowing refugees to return to their homes. The relations between Greece and the Ottoman Empire threatened to erupt into war in 1914. It was over the forcible expulsion of Greeks from Thrace and the western shores of Asia Minor by the Turks and Turks from Epirus and Macedonia by the Greeks. Furthermore, the Turks boycotted Greek businesses throughout the empire.

The Ecumenical Patriarch ordered all churches and schools closed as a protest to the deportations and boycott. He petitioned the Sultan for his intervention on this matter but his request was ignored. I received a call from the Patriarch asking me to use my good offices since the US was highly regarded and respected in Constantinople and Athens. I told him that we didn't intervene in the internal affairs of other nations.

Then came the turn of the Greek ambassador, Nikolaos Papanastasis requesting the assistance of our government regarding the expulsion of his compatriots. I explained that whilst we were sympathetic to their plight but our neutrality didn't allow us to intervene in this crisis. However, we suggested to the Turks to arrange with the Greeks to stop the deportations. Papanastasis later told me that Greek premier, Venizelos and Grand Vizier, Ahmed Riza Pasha agreed to a voluntary exchange of populations including the creation of a mixed commission to settle abandoned properties and compensation claims. I thought this was a wonderful idea defusing a potential conflict situation.

War broke out in Europe in August 1914, the Turks announced their neutrality which I knew wasn't true. I learned from various sources that they had concluded a secret agreement with the Germans to enter the war of a time of their choosing. Some three months later, the Ottoman navy commanded by German admiral, Souchon shelled Russian naval positions in the Black Sea. Washington instructed me to maintain cordial relations with the Young Turks. We needed to protect our schools, hospitals, and orphanages that operated in the empire. Our missionaries were always careful to ensure that both Christians and Muslims were treaty equally and fairly.

I was receiving reports from our Consuls and missionaries regarding the deportation and massacres of Armenians and Greeks in Asia Minor. I kept Washington informed of these developments and asked them whether I should protest the Grand Vizier. The answer was YES. I arranged a meeting with Enver Pasha and told him that our government's position regarding the deportations and massacres.

"The Greeks and Armenians have conspired with our enemies and are being relocated to safety zones", Enver stated. "The US is most unhappy with the deportations and massacres which is harming your empire's reputation", I said. He denied massacres were taking place but his government did everything to protect them from reprisals. I didn't believe him. I confronted him with evidence of massacres but again he denied it. There was very little I could do to help these poor souls.

I was recalled to Washington in November 1916 ending the most eventful diplomatic post of them all. A post filled with conflict and death. I was glad to be back in the US thinking about the fate of the Greeks and Armenians and also our missionary activity in Turkey.

www.ingramcontent.com/pod-product-compliance
Lightning Source LLC
Chambersburg PA
CBHW021627120626
46545CB00002B/441